CURVED STRIP–PIECING

A NEW TECHNIQUE

Marilyn Stothers

PH PRESS
WINNIPEG
MANITOBA
CANADA

This book is dedicated to my mother Margaret Christie Stewart,
my father William J. A. Stewart, and my husband Stephen Stothers, all educators.

Copyright 1988 by Marilyn Stothers

Front Cover: Detail – <u>Curving Cubes I</u>
                 53″/135 cm × 55″/140 cm
                 by Marilyn Stothers

Back Cover: <u>Curving Cubes I</u>

Photography: Marilyn Stothers
                 Ernest Mayer

Illustrations: Marilyn Stothers

Printer: Friesen Printers

Published by: PH Press
                 c/o Marilyn Stothers
                 85 Agassiz Drive
                 Winnipeg, Manitoba
                 Canada R3T 2K9

Copies of this book may be ordered from the above address

Printed in Canada

ISBN 0–88925–899–6

CONTENTS

ACKNOWLEDGEMENTS

This book would not have been possible without the support and encouragement of many people.

First and foremost, I owe a great deal to my students who, not knowing in the beginning what Curved Strip–Piecing was, have signed up to take classes. To them I express thanks for their faith and pioneering spirit. Their enthusiasm and input, especially the suggestions of Isobel Johnson and Lou Olson, have greatly encouraged my continued exploration into this new technique, and my belief that Curved Strip–Piecing is a valid method of assembling fabric for quiltmaking. I should point out to earlier students that they should check this book for changes that have clarified and improved the methods of Curved Strip–Piecing as I now use them – changes that were inevitable when one is developing something new!

Special thanks are due:

To Helen Russell whose expertise as a computer whiz, quiltmaker and former magazine editor has been and will continue to be invaluable;

To friends and colleagues who have asked, ''When is your book coming out??'' which has pushed me to do something about it;

To conference and guild program planners who have given me the opportunity to teach Curved Strip–Piecing Workshops when the technique was and is so new;

To quiltmakers who have sent pictures and slides of their work using Curved Strip–Piecing;

To my family for their support and belief in individual freedoms;

And especially to my husband, Steve, who continues to encourage me in my ongoing work as well as in my teaching.

BEGINNINGS

In my contemporary quiltmaking I have been using the technique of strip–piecing to achieve a desired pieced surface design. In 1977, I was reading about and studying the work of an American painter, Ellsworth Kelly, who in the 1950's had painted an abstract work and decided to rearrange his canvas by tearing it into strips at random, then reassembling those strips into an arrangement of blocks similar in appearance to the block/grid system of quiltmaking. This caused me to wonder what would happen if one treated fabric in much the same way to make new meterage/yardage. However, several layers of fabric would have to be randomly 'stripped' and reassembled in such a way that the joining seams would match or fit. It is one thing to use paper and glue, but another to use woven fabric and the sewing machine.

With this in mind, I took about a metre (or yard) of two different coloured broadcloths, experimenting by layering one on top of the other, and then curve cutting long fabric strips in a freehand motion. I separated the curved strips, alternating the two colours, and sewed them together. The result was two new pieces of fabric – each stripped alternately with the two colours used. The strips, however, were not uniformly straight – they were gently curved, some areas wide and some narrow. These became the first curved strip–pieced bands.

My first quilt using this technique of Curved Strip–Piecing, <u>Heaven and Earth</u>, was pieced in 1978. However, the quilting was not finished until 1982 when I decided to devote myself again full–time to my quiltmaking, after having owned a quilt shop in the four intervening years. My experimentation with Curved Strip–Piecing continued. In 1983, my <u>Discoveries</u> quilt, and the jacket assembled from leftover pieces of this quilt, further explored and refined this new technique (see colour pages).

As I have worked with Curved Strip–Piecing one additional feature has become very apparent. My scissors have become my drawing tool. Usually in quiltmaking scissors are taken for granted – they cut fabric. But in Curved Strip–Piecing they do more than that. This technique requires that you freehand cut curves around guideline measuring marks. The direction of cutting, i.e. the progression of curves, the configuration, etc., is decided as you cut. There is no need to pre–plan or to follow a pencil and paper drawing. It requires thinking as you work and becomes a challenge to achieve the best possible arrangement of curves within a strip band – by using your scissors.

I continue to experiment, and today I am finding fresh and interesting ways to use Curved Strip–Piecing in each new project. My Reflections and Illusions series of five quilts and the Curving Cubes series (two quilts to date) all used Curved Strip–Piecing in some part of the surface design. The third quilt in my Assimilation series used straight strip–pieced bands as fabrics which were then cut in the Curved Strip–Piecing technique as a design element. My quilt in the new Fabricvisions series, ''Mommy, Will There Always be Flowers?'' 1986, uses Curved Strip–Piecing for dimensional and descriptive purposes. (See colour pages.)

There are as many ways to use Curved Strip–Piecing in fabric work as there are creative ideas from each fabric artist. The artist/quiltmaker who is concerned with finding a technique which manipulates fabric to produce curving or rounded images for a project should seriously consider Curved Strip–Piecing for this purpose.

INTRODUCTION
TO CURVED STRIP–PIECING

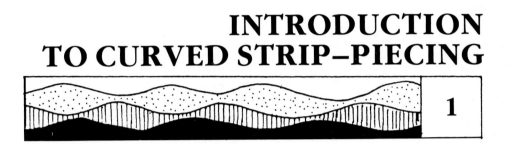

Today's quiltmakers and fabric artists are adventuresome people willing to try new designs, new fabrics and new techniques. The designs may be traditional with a new twist, i.e. colour, size, placement. The fabrics may not always be 100% cotton, i.e. polyester/cotton, silk, satin, velvet. The techniques may require a sewing machine, even machine quilting. There are many choices and many combinations. That is what makes working with fabric so special, so challenging and so individual. Curved Strip–Piecing comes from this freedom.

I was working with straight strip–piecing and wondered what would happen if instead of cutting 'straight' strips of fabric, I deliberately cut 'curved' strips. I could cut them but what were the complications of sewing them together? From this questioning, Curved Strip–Piecing was born.

As I explored the possibilities of this new technique of strip–piecing, I found that two methods of cutting and assembling the curved strips were needed. If there was no specific planned order in the appearance of colour, strip widths, or patterns of fabric next to each other in the finished strip band, then I used a method for cutting the fabrics I call RANDOM Curved Strip–Piecing. However, if there was a pre–arranged scheme to follow, i.e. sequential colours of the rainbow, colour values, lights to darks, or increasing or decreasing widths of strips, etc., then I had to use another system of cutting fabrics which I call GRADATED Curved Strip–Piecing. In all, the most important fact to bear in mind is that each curved strip must fit into the curves of the next strip to which it is sewn. In all Curved Strip–Piecing, the strips once cut are not interchangeable, may not be trimmed or altered in shape, and must always fit only in the sequence cut. Where one strip has a convex curve, the other must have a corresponding concave curve to fit into, and vice versa. That is the secret of Curved Strip–Piecing – the cutting and assembling.

As you read this book and work through the methods described, you will have a tendency to compare the Curved Strip–Piecing methods with straight strip–piecing. The end use is the same, the principle is the same,

1

but the marking, cutting and assembling are different. The Curved Strip–Piecing methods will take slightly longer in cutting and piecing time, but are less structured. In quiltmaking, especially in piecework, we are always conscious of being totally accurate. 'Accuracy' is a most important element in good design. This rule still holds and always will; except that in Curved Strip–Piecing the cutting and sewing together of the curved strips allow for some freedom and flexibility. This will become apparent to you as you work through the directions for the methods of Curved Strip–Piecing. Be prepared to let yourself go with this more unstructured technique!

I have purposely not discussed the basic steps in quiltmaking. There are many fine reference books which give complete instruction and 'how-to'. This book will teach you how to master the technique of strip–piecing with curves. As I taught many workshops in different parts of North America, I was asked by students if there was a book on Curved Strip–Piecing they could use for reference, and by teachers who wanted a book to supplement their classes. This manual on Curved Strip–Piecing is the result.

DEFINITION

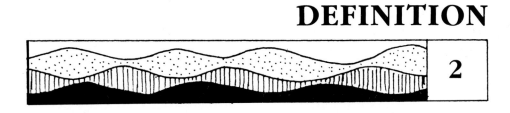

What exactly is Curved Strip–Piecing?? What does it look like?

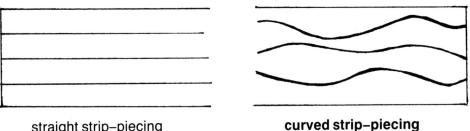

straight strip–piecing   **curved strip–piecing**

Figure 2.1

To discuss Curved Strip–Piecing one has to define strip–piecing in general. Strip–piecing is the process of sewing together long strips of fabric of varying widths and colour sequences to make new fabric or meterage/yardage as the basis for creating the surface design that is planned.

The difference between straight strips and curved strips is mainly the cutting. Straight strips of uniform width are cut most often by a sharp rotary cutter in straight, parallel lines and accurately sewn together in straight seams giving the appearance of sharp, geometric, hard, static outlines. Curved strips are also made from long pieces of fabric but the strips are freehand cut with scissors in gentle curves in a system that allows each strip to 'fit into' these curves and be sewn together – like putting together a jigsaw puzzle. The finished curved strip–pieced band in appearance will have soft gentle curves, a wavy fluid motion. Using templates, component fabric pieces are cut from this newly–made fabric which when sewn together produce the planned finished design.

When working with fabric, curves have traditionally been surface appliquéd or reverse appliquéd, or have been cut from a curve–shaped template or flexible tool, and then pieced very carefully with great control and accuracy. With Curved Strip–Piecing there is now an additional option of adding curves to your design. Many times a series of curves is needed, or the effect of sky or water, or an ethereal feeling of softness, or the use of negative and positive images. All these and many more design possibilities can be explored using Curved Strip–Piecing. As always, imagination has no limits. To my knowledge, this is a new technique that has not been used before. It is not replacing any previous method, but should be considered an additional way of manipulating fabric for new surface design. Straight strip–piecing with fabric has been around for a long time as an effective visual designing tool. Now you will learn another way to make strip–piecing – Curved Strip–Piecing.

DISCUSSION OF METHODS

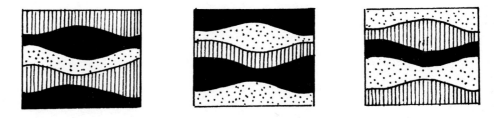

3

There are two methods of constructing Curved Strip–Piecing. As I worked with designing I realized that there are times when the order of the stripping, i.e. the placement of one strip next to the other, could be unplanned or at random. At other times a definite order was required to get the effect desired in the overall design. This meant that the procedure of cutting the fabrics had to be different. After much experimenting, two methods evolved.

METHOD I – RANDOM Curved Strip–Piecing

The first method developed I call RANDOM Curved Strip–Piecing. In the finished stripped band the placing of colour, of patterns, of varying widths, is haphazard or unplanned in arrangement; there is no specific order. It is the easier of the two methods and less time–consuming as far as the actual cutting of the fabrics is concerned. To achieve the RANDOM effect, multiple layers of stacked fabric are cut, the strips are separated, then reassembled in a cutting order but a random placement, and sewn together. When the sewing is finished, the RANDOM Curved Strip–Piecing method makes several (depending on the number of fabrics selected) stripped bands from the initial cutting resulting in varying combinations with which to work in surface designing.

RANDOM curved strip–piecing — 3 fabrics

Figure 3.1

METHOD II – GRADATED Curved Strip–Piecing

The second method is named GRADATED Curved Strip–Piecing. This method is used when there is a planned, specific arrangement of the strip–piecing in the design project. It may be a controlled gradation of colours either in a monochromatic or polychromatic order; it may be a series of varying widths such as wide to narrow, or strips that alternate wide and narrow. There are many ways an ordered scheme may be planned. The process for cutting the fabric is more complex. In the GRADATED method, after assembling there will be less finished meterage/ yardage than with the RANDOM method of cutting because only one layer of each fabric is cut at a time.

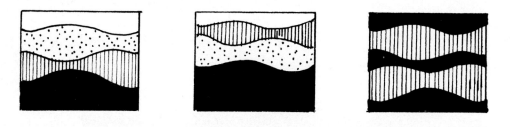

GRADATED **curved strip–piecing — 3 arrangements**

Figure 3.2

With two methods of Curved Strip–Piecing from which to choose, it becomes evident that as a designer and planner, before selecting the fabrics and method of construction, you must decide what effect you want visually from your finished strip bands. Do you want an orderly arrangement; do you want a casual grouping; do you want colour gradation; do you want the effects of both RANDOM and GRADATED Curved Strip–Piecing in your project? You may also consider using the two strippiecing techniques, i.e. both straight and curved, effectively in the same plan. There are many choices to make. They will decide which of the two methods you follow for marking and cutting the fabrics.

Because Curved Strip–Piecing is new and you use scissors as a drawing tool to cut curves, which does take some practice, you may feel more comfortable learning with construction paper first. Work with paper in much the same way most of us learned Seminole patchwork. I use this method in my workshops because it is difficult to learn to be free with fabric when you are not used to it.

EQUIPMENT

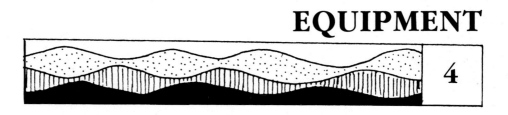

4

The most important tools to have are your sewing machine, your scissors – and your imagination!

Sewing Machine:

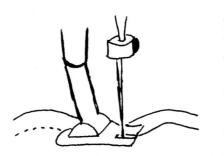

Curved Strip–Piecing is best sewn by sewing machine (hand–seaming would not be practical or strong enough), and only requires a machine that straight stitches – no multi–stitch machine is needed. However, your sewing machine should be in perfect order, with even tension and stitching. You must know how to feed fabric under the needle and presser foot carefully and with skill (practice makes perfect!). If your machine speed can be reduced, setting it at the slower speed will help you control the seaming and slight manipulation of the strips. As you sew the strips together it is very important to handle gently but guide the fabrics firmly with no additional pressure or tension.

Scissors:

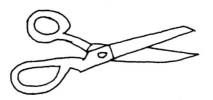

Your fabric scissors must be sharp and easy to handle. They are your drawing tool. Not only are your scissors performing the important task of separating fabric(s) into strips by shearing, but they are freehand drawing and designing curving lines as you wield them from fold to selvedge. This action should not be without thought, i.e. just going through the motions of cutting, because as you cut the inner strips especially (those not on the outside edge) you are purposely aware of and trying to design, manipulate, 'draw', cut opposing curves to the configuration already cut in the preceding strip. If you like a challenge, you will find one in cutting curved strip–pieces!

Sharp scissors are necessary to cut through multiple layers of fabrics. They should be sharp enough not to 'drag' or pull the fabrics one over the other out of order. Some of my students have suggested using a rotary cutter. You may wish to try this if you are skillful with cutting layers of fabric and have great control over your cutter. But for the reasons stated, I prefer to use my scissors. I find that by holding my fabrics in one hand and using the scissors in the other I have greater control in designing and 'drawing' curves as I cut.

Pins:

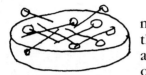

In straight strip–piecing pins are not always necessary. However, in Curved Strip–Piecing I find that pins are necessary at strategic places when you assemble the strips. As you read through the methods you will find that I pin where my 'hills' and 'valleys' meet all across the strip so that the meeting of convex and concave curves does not get out of control, my strips are not stretched, and the strips meet and sew together properly. Long plastic–headed pins are best for this. (See STEP 6 – D. 2) <u>Pinning.</u>)

Ruler:

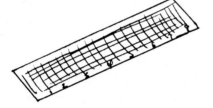

A plastic ruler, one you can see through, is very valuable in measuring the approximate width of strip you wish to cut, and for using as a guide in the random marking of the fabric across the strip, marking which will guide the scissors when you are cut–ting. Being able to see through the ruler also allows you to see the outline of the curving formation of the previously cut strip.

Marking Pencils or Equivalent:

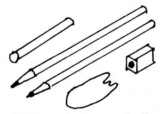

Use a dark marker, i.e. disappearing pencil or coloured pencil, for light fabrics and a light marker, i.e. chalk, soapstone, soap slivers, for dark fabrics. With the Curved Strip–Piecing technique, you will be marking guideline measurements on the RIGHT side of the fabric, marks around which your scissors will cut. These 'signposts' should be as inconspicuous as possible, so choose carefully the markers you use.

Thread:

Choose a good quality sewing thread, one that works well in your machine. The colour should be one that blends well with all the colours of the fabrics you are using. It should not need to be changed as you go from colour to colour unless you are using a range of light to dark colours or values. Then you may prefer to change the thread to blend accordingly. A mid–value of grey works well with most colour and fabric com–binations. If your machine tension is perfect, the thread will sink into the fabric and the colour will not be particularly noticeable.

Fabrics:

The best fabric to use with Curved Strip–Piecing is 100% cotton. Cotton has a flexibility in seaming and especially in pressing that is advantageous when working with curves. A fabric blend of polyester and cotton is acceptable. Usually 65% polyester/35% cotton is available in most stores. If you have a choice of 50% polyester/50% cotton or better, the higher percentage of cotton is preferable. It is best to use fabrics that are firmly woven and wash well, are medium weight, colourfast and easy–to–iron. The easiest fabrics to work with are the broadcloths. All fabrics should be pre–washed, pre–shrunk in the same manner that they will be treated in the finished project. The widths may vary from 90 cm to 140 cm (35/36″ to 54″). That does not matter as this method of cutting curves in strip–piecing works from the centre of the fabric, i.e. the fold, toward the selvedges. (See STEP 6 – B. Cutting the Strips.)

It is possible to use other fabrics. If you wish to use silk or velvet or any other exotic material, you know before you do the problems you will encounter, i.e. fraying edges which will require increased seam allowances, and bulky fabric combinations which may be difficult to machine stitch and press, etc. If you decide to use such fabrics, try a sample in the Curved Strip–Piecing method first. Do not use these fabrics in a 'beginner's' project. Know the technique well first. These fabrics require a skill with the sewing machine as well.

In RANDOM Curved Strip–Piecing you may choose to use all plain fabrics, all print fabrics or a combination of both. A small all–over design works best for print fabrics because special effects from larger directional or graphic prints may be lost in the varying widths of the strips, as well as mask the curving shape cut. As you become very experienced at Curved Strip–Piecing you may wish to try such unusual fabrics.

Colour:

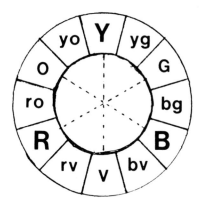

Analogous colour mixtures, i.e. those colours close to each other on the colour wheel, make an effective visual presence when used together in various combinations. The same is true for values of one colour or complementary colours in the same values. Varying the strip widths as well as the colours in the RANDOM method will add variety to the finished design because of the multiple cutting system and random visual order in assembling. In the GRADATED method colours can be used very effectively. You may wish to use a sequence of values of light to dark of one colour for spatial illusion. The width of each strip can also be controlled in a sequential order. You would use this method for any planned arrangement with colours and/or fabrics.

NOTES

THE BASIC Curved Strip–Piecing FORMULA for Both Methods

5

When using Curved Strip–Piecing, I have found it easier to follow a set plan of action. There are six steps to my <u>Basic Curved Strip–Piecing Formula</u>. These steps are listed below in order of procedure and each will be discussed later in detail.

STEP 1: Decide how the Curved Strip–Piecing is to be used in your work. Decide which Curved Strip–Piecing method (RANDOM or GRADATED) you wish to use to produce the surface design you are planning.

STEP 2: Select the fabrics required for the chosen design effect.

STEP 3: Determine the total measurement of the finished width of your desired strip–pieced band(s).

STEP 4: Decide on (A) the number of strips you wish within this strip–pieced band. Calculate (B) the approximate finished width of each curved strip within the band (remember that you are dealing with curves). These measurements, when added together, give you the finished measurement as selected in STEP 3.
For instance, each strip may a) be similar in width measurement
  b) increase in width from narrow to wide
  c) vary in width
  d) alternate wide and narrow, etc.

STEP 5: To each strip measurement from STEP 4, add the seam allowances, plus
  – for the RANDOM method, add the DESIGNING FACTOR (see detailed description on page 18) to each <u>outside</u> strip ONLY (the first and last strips in the band);
  – for the GRADATED method, add the DESIGNING FACTOR (see detailed description on page 18) to <u>all</u> strips.
These calculations provide guidelines for the marking and cut–

ting of your fabrics. Note these measurements on paper for reference.

STEP 6: Follow the directions for either the RANDOM or GRADATED method of Curved Strip–Piecing.
A. Marking the Strips – Outer and Inner
B. Cutting the Strips
C. Preparing the Strips for Sewing
D. Sewing the Strips Together to Form the Strip Band
E. Pressing the Strip Band
F. Marking, Cutting and Sewing Design Shapes

Many of the steps in the Basic Curved Strip–Piecing Formula will seem to occur simultaneously in the decision–making process, so do not feel that each must be absolutely resolved before you proceed to the next. The Basic Formula provides guidelines for you to adapt to your own way of planning before you actually cut and sew. However, it is important to make the necessary mathematical calculations and to know the direction you are taking before you mark and cut into your fabrics.

STEP 1

Decide on the basic idea or concept you wish to use for this new project. Are you going to make curved strip–pieced band(s) on which you will place template shapes, i.e. squares, triangles, etc., cut them out and then reassemble into your design pattern? Do you intend to use uncut long curved strip–pieced band(s) for a special effect?

Using the descriptions of the two methods of Curved Strip–Piecing (RANDOM and GRADATED) already discussed, decide which method your project requires. If you want an overall effect of colours or shapes in your design with no particular visual organization, use the RANDOM Curved Strip–Piecing method. If you want a planned progression of colours or colour values, or width measurements, etc., use the GRA-DATED method of Curved Strip–Piecing.

You have now made the first decisions – the direction you are going to take in designing your work, and the technique which will help you achieve that result. Now on to STEP 2.

STEP 2

The selection of fabrics is a challenging task!! At this point I usually gather my fabrics around me and try to make decisions. Sometimes nar-rowing an idea down to one specific direction, i.e. colours, and selecting the right fabrics to express that image, are the hardest parts of the quiltmaking process! The fabric selection does not have to be absolutely final at this point. You may find you need to add a special colour that would highlight the colours you have, or a lighter or darker value of one colour that would bridge the transition from one area to another. Play with your fabrics until the arrangement is pleasing to the eye and conveys the mental image you have of your design.

In selecting fabrics for the GRADATED method you are looking for a planned arrangement, a specific order, for those fabrics. Place the fabrics next to each other in the order you envision in the final strip–pieced band. That will help you to make choices. Rearrange them until you are satisfied.

In the RANDOM method the fabrics will not be in any specific order, so it is necessary to choose fabrics that go well together no matter what their order. You need to play with your choices, move them around so that you can see all the possible permutations and combinations, and be satisfied that the fabrics you finally choose will work in a random or visually unplanned manner. These decisions in general should be made before proceeding to STEP 3.

STEP 3

Calculate the desired finished measurement of the width of the curved strip–pieced band(s) you need to make for your design. Work with paper and pencil.

EXAMPLE: If your design requires 4″ squares and you use a 4″ square (finished measurement) template, then you know that the finished width measurement of the strip–pieced band must be a minimum of 4″ to which a ¼″ seam allowance is added to each side, to equal 4½″ total minimum width measurement. I use the word 'minimum' because I like to have my outside edges wider (by adding additional seam allowance to those edges) to accommodate moving my template up and down slightly across the finished band to achieve different effects. This additional seam allowance, to the outside band edges, I call the DESIGNING FACTOR. It will be fully described in STEP 5.

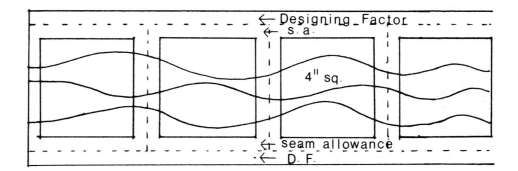

Curved strip–pieced band for 4 inch sq. template

Figure 5.1

STEP 4

Now you must decide the following:
A) the number of curved strips you need within the finished strip–pieced band
B) the approximate finished width measurement of each strip
   Also, this will indicate the number of fabrics required from the fabrics selected in STEP 2. You may have already decided the number of strips at the same time as you selected your fabrics, some decisions are simultaneous. If you have not made a final choice and are still undecided, consider whether to use two or more fabrics only once each, to repeat the use of one or more fabrics, or to have a number of different colour and/or patterned fabrics, etc.

A) The Number of Curved Strips
RANDOM Curved Strip–Piecing Method

If you plan to use the RANDOM Curved Strip–Piecing method, layering allows for multiple cuts of the fabrics. Remember the word 'random' means an unplanned visual order of fabric, colour, etc., within the finished band. In this method it is most important to calculate the number of strips you wish to have within the band. This will be evident when you cut your fabrics. The RANDOM method is also the one to use if you wish to have two fabrics only in a repetitive sequence.

EXAMPLE: You may require a strip band of 4″ plus seam allowance with which to work (STEP 3). In the planning stage, you have the choice of breaking up that finished 4″ into two strips, three, four, possibly five strips. Any more would make the strips too narrow to cut or sew. The idea is to divide the four inches into workable sections to cut and assemble. If you decide on two strips, you may choose two fabrics; if three strips, you may wish to use three fabrics; if four strips, you may select four different fabrics or you may choose other combinations. In the RANDOM method, where the fabrics are layered or stacked on top of one another, each time the fabrics are cut, all layers are cut in a curved strip at the same time. Each fabric will have an identical curved strip. This allows for a random order of placing because the next strips cut will also have an identical strip of each fabric. Therefore, you can plan to cut as many sets of curved strips as you wish and to vary their placement in each strip band.

EXAMPLE: Using two fabrics, you may have decided to have four strips of approximately equal width, i.e. 1″ strips, in the curved strip–pieced band. This equals a finished 4″ band. The two fabrics are layered one on top of the other, and cut in the Curved Strip–Piecing technique four times (once for each strip) – the first three cuts are curved, the last one is straight.

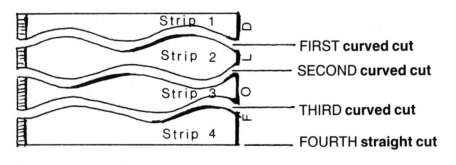

Figure 5.2

Because you have cut a stacked layer of two fabrics you have cut enough for two finished bands the length of the fabric widths used, all at the same time. When the fabrics are separated and assembled, this is what you will have:

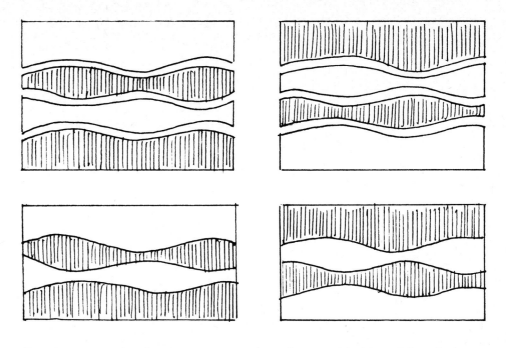

Random curved strips cut, separated, and assembled into 2 bands from two fabrics

Figure 5.3

If you invert Band 2 you will have the same order of strips, and have two bands that are similar and could be joined end–to–end to make one very long strip band for a special purpose such as an expanse of sea or sky.

EXAMPLE: The same could be done with three fabrics. This time there are to be five strips in the design. The three fabrics are stacked one on top of the other and the 5 strips are marked with the guideline measurements calculated. (See STEP 6 – A. <u>Marking the Strips</u>.) Then they are cut, the first four cuts being curved and the fifth one straight. This time when the fabric strips are separated, because there are three fabrics there will be three strip bands ready for assembling. With three fabrics every curved cut is in triplicate. When the fabrics are separated and assembled this is what you will have:

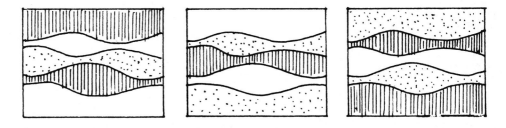

RANDOM curved strip–pieced bands assembled from 3 fabrics

Figure 5.4

Note that the fabric placement is random and each finished band appears different although you use the same fabrics. It is important to remember that in Curved Strip–Piecing the strips once cut are <u>not</u> inter–

changeable. Each strip cut has a specific order for fitting the contours of the strip cut next to it – like a jigsaw puzzle. The strips must not be trimmed, reshaped or altered after the initial cutting.

The RANDOM Curved Strip–Piecing method differs greatly from straight strip–piecing. The multiple layering and cutting of strips produces several stripped bands at the same time. The number of bands produced will depend on the number of fabrics used. Three fabrics yield three bands, four fabrics yield four bands, etc. However, I have found that an uneven number of fabrics, i.e. three or five (more fabrics become cumber–some to manipulate and require very sharp scissors to cut accurately), results in a more pleasing mixture of colours and final appearance than an even number. You will also note that the number of strips you need for your strip–pieced band is the number of cuts you will need to make. If you need four strips, you will make three curved cuts and one straight cut. The curved cuts are the curves within your strip, the straight cut is the straight outside edge of the last strip.

As you practise and become familiar with the RANDOM Curved Strip–Piecing method, you may vary and manipulate the number of fab–rics, number of strips, and order of placement in any way you wish. You must always remember to keep to the order of cutting. The first curved strip cut will only 'fit' the second curved strip, which 'fits' the third curved strip, etc. This order must always be maintained or you will have chaos!

GRADATED Curved Strip–Piecing Method

The GRADATED method is a planned arrangement of strips. When you are using this method of Curved Strip–Piecing, you deliberately plan the specific order of your strips. The order has to do with width measurements, colour sequences, etc., of each strip, all to give you the effect you are planning.

Select the fabrics you wish to use and arrange them in the correct sequence. Decide if you need to make any changes to give you the effect you seek. As in all Curved Strip–Piecing these strips, once cut, are not interchangeable so you must be very sure of your order before you cut. When you have arranged the fabrics in the best sequence for your design you will also have an indication of the number of strips (depending on the width of the band) you will need. Make the mathematical calculations on paper before you mark and cut. This time the fabrics will be cut one fabric strip at a time (this is different from the RANDOM method where all the fabrics are stacked and cut at one time). The result will be that when all the strips are cut, there will be the exact number of strips you need to assemble into one curved strip–pieced band.

SELVEDGES

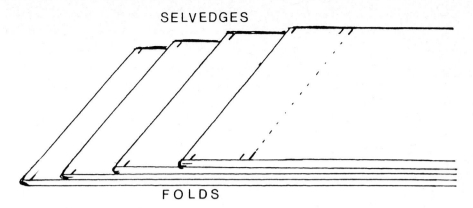

FOLDS

Each fabric measured and marked for GRADATED curved strip–piecing

Figure 5.5a

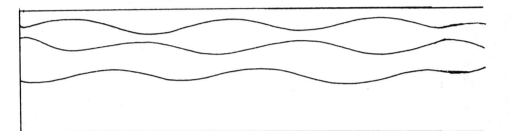

One completed GRADATED curved strip-pieced band — each strip a different width

Figure 5.5b

B) Finished Width Measurement of Each Strip

Calculate on paper the approximate finished width (remember you are creating curves) of each curved strip which makes up the band. These measurements when added together give you the measurement decided in STEP 3.

Now is the time to decide if you want your curved strips to be similar in width measurement, or vary in measurement in specific progression, etc. These measurement figures are to act as guidelines when you cut the curves.

RANDOM Curved Strip–Piecing Method

The width of the finished strip band helps you decide the measurement of each strip.

EXAMPLE: If the finished width is 4″, then the finished widths of the individual strips together must total 4″. The four inches can be divided into four strips of 1″ each (4″ total), or four strips of varying widths such as ³/₄″, 1″, 1¹/₄″, 1″ (again 4″ total). Any measurements may be used as long as the width is not narrower than ¹/₂″. Because of seam allowances and difficulty in handling for beginners, ¹/₂″ is the safest narrow measurement. If you become experienced you may experiment with widths less than ¹/₂″. You may also consider dividing the 4″ band into two or three strips, always adding up the measurements selected for each strip to total a finished 4″. Remember that you work with the finished measurements first. The next step, STEP 5, will add the seam allowances.

GRADATED Curved Strip–Piecing Method

The GRADATED method of calculating the finished width measurements of each strip is much the same, except that you have a definite plan in mind.

EXAMPLE: If the finished band is to be 5″ wide and composed of gradually widening strips, the strips might be ½″, ¾″, 1″, 1¼″ and 1½″. The total width of the strips is 5″. Perhaps you might want to alternate wide and narrow bands, i.e. 1″, 1½″, 1″ and 1½″, to total 5″. There are many possible combinations to help you achieve the design you want. Be sure to note all your calculations on paper so that it will be easier to add seam allowances to each strip in the next step, STEP 5.

STEP 5

In Curved Strip–Piecing the addition of seam allowances to the strips will give the guidelines for marking and cutting your fabrics. You have now made calculations on paper for the required width of the finished stripped band, for the number of strips that make up that band, and the average finished width measurement of each strip. Now is the time to add the seam allowance measurements to each strip. Then you will be ready to mark and cut!

As in all quiltmaking you add the usual seam allowance of ¼″ to each side of the strip in calculating the measurements for marking and cutting. However, in Curved Strip–Piecing, there is as well, the addition of the DESIGNING FACTOR which differs with each method. In the RANDOM method, the addition of the DESIGNING FACTOR is to the outside edges only of the first and last strips in the planned band. In the GRADATED method, the addition of the DESIGNING FACTOR is to all the strips in the planned band.

RANDOM Method – Inner Strips

To the average finished measurements of each inner strip, add ¼″ seam allowance to each side of the strip. For example, to the average finished strip width of 1″, add ¼″ + ¼″ = ½″, for a marking and cutting measurement of 1½″. When sewn, the average finished width measurement should be 1″ as calculated in STEP 4.

RANDOM Method – Outer Strips
GRADATED Method – All Strips (Inner and Outer)

To each of the <u>outer</u> strips in the RANDOM Curved Strip–Piecing method, and to <u>all</u> the strips in the GRADATED method add ¼″ + ¼″ = ½″ seam allowances. In addition, as indicated in STEP 4, these seam allowance measurements are increased by what I have termed the DESIGNING FACTOR.

THE DESIGNING FACTOR

The DESIGNING FACTOR is the addition of a minimum of ½″ to the seam allowance on one edge only of the indicated strips. The DESIGNING

FACTOR is added to the calculated measurements and the total amount becomes the marking–for–cutting guideline of the above designated strips in Curved Strip–Piecing.

When measuring the <u>outer</u> strips in the RANDOM and the GRA–DATED methods – add ½″ DESIGNING FACTOR to the outside or unsewn band edges.

For example, if the approximate finished width desired for an outer strip is 1″, add the usual seam allowances of ¼″ + ¼″ = ½″; the width is now 1½″. To this add the DESIGNING FACTOR of ½″ to the outside seam edge only. The total width of the strip for marking and cutting is now:

1″	– finished width
½″	– seam allowances of ¼″ + ¼″
½″	– DESIGNING FACTOR
2″	– TOTAL

When measuring the <u>inner</u> strips for the GRADATED method, add ½″ DESIGNING FACTOR to the 'left' edge only of each strip (if you work from left to right).

For example, if the approximate finished width desired for each inner strip is 1″, add the usual seam allowances of ¼″ + ¼″ = ½″ to each; the width is now 1½″. To this add the DESIGNING FACTOR of ½″ to the 'left' seam edge only. The total width measurement of each inner strip for marking and cutting is now:

1″	– finished width
½″	– seam allowances of ¼″ + ¼″
½″	– DESIGNING FACTOR
2″	– TOTAL

There are four good reasons for the DESIGNING FACTOR:

1. Adding a minimum of ½″ to the outside seam allowance of ¼″ increases the width of this edge of the band and will compensate for any loss in the finished width measurement due to the machine sewing of the curves of the inner strip seams. This additional allowance also builds in a cushion for any deviation, through calculating error or otherwise, from the planned guidelines of STEP 1 in the Curved Strip–Piecing Formula. Curving strips of fabric, depending on the depth of the curves, when sewn together do not produce a completely uniform measurement across each band as in straight strip–piecing. In fact, you are striving for this difference!

2. Adding to the seam allowance builds in a margin of 'creative licence' for working with your templates later. I often add more than ½″. This is why in defining the DESIGNING FACTOR I have said 'a minimum of ½″'. In Curved Strip–Piecing you are working with long, uneven curved lines which are wide in some areas and narrow in others; there is a wide diversification of line as you look at the finished strip band. When placing your template on the band you may wish to raise it, lower it, or move it to take advantage of the most interesting curves or contrasting movements. Having that extra fabric at the top and bottom of the band allows for this flexibility and design freedom. The result will also enhance the surface image of your work.

3. Adding the DESIGNING FACTOR to the seam allowance on the outside edges is good practice as you will see once you have become adept at using and visualizing curves in Curved Strip–Piecing. You may wish

to join one curved strip–pieced band to another so that the joining seam will also be curved strip–pieced. To do this, you need the extra fabric in the seam allowances. Each band is treated as you do a 'fabric', layering one on top of the other as the directions for GRADATED Curved Strip–Piecing indicate, and cutting a curving line which you can then seam. It is only possible to do this if there is enough additional fabric to work with on the outside edges or first and last strips of the curved strip–pieced bands.

NOTE:An increase to the outside seam allowance might be worth thinking about in straight strip–piecing as well if you wish more leeway in designing.

4. Adding the ½″ DESIGNING FACTOR to the inner strip measurements of GRADATED Curved Strip–Piecing only is a crucial part of that method to establish a guideline for cutting the strips. The GRADATED method does not use multiple layers of fabrics. In this method each selected fabric is cut one at a time, so it is necessary to have a measurement which allows for overlapping the fabrics without diminishing seam allowances.

In summing up STEPS 4 and 5, in general any width not less than a finished measurement of ½″ is possible for each strip; very narrow strips will create problems with the bulk of seam allowances on the back. In Curved Strip–Piecing these measurements are to be used as guidelines for marking and cutting only because you are not dealing with straight lines. The curving lines or contours of your strips will be narrow in some places and wide in others – this is what you want. Keep in mind that the width of the strips should be in scale with the templates to be cut from them and with the planned design. The DESIGNING FACTOR is used in both the RANDOM and GRADATED Curved Strip–Piecing methods.

STEP 6

A. Marking the Strips
1) Outer Strips
In STEP 5 I talked about the DESIGNING FACTOR and the reasons for adding this additional seam allowance to the outer edges of the outside strips in both RANDOM and GRADATED Curved Strip–Piecing methods.

The outer strips, i.e. the first and last strips cut, each have one straight edge and one curved edge. In the former, the curved edge results from the first cut of the fabrics in the first strip, and in the latter, from the last curving cut before the straight cut of the last strip. The straight edges are the outside edges of those strips. It is to this straight outside edge that the DESIGNING FACTOR of ½″ is added. This is in addition to the ¼″ + ¼″ = ½″ usual seam allowance measurements. If your outer strip is to be 1″ approximate finished measurement, then add ¼″ + ¼″ = ½″ plus the DESIGNING FACTOR of ½″. The total measurement to use a guideline for marking and cutting your fabric is now 2″.

2) Inner Strips
In Curved Strip–Piecing marking the width of strips from the calculated measurements gives a guideline to use visually as you freehand cut the curves. You may wonder then why you took the time to figure

out all those measurements if you are not going to follow them exactly. As in all prior planning for a specific project, you have an idea of spaces to fill and ways to work with shapes. It would be a waste of time to throw something together quickly without measuring, hoping it would work, and then find the proportion was all wrong, the placement of colours and shapes would not work, etc. In Curved Strip–Piecing time must be taken for planning. Then you have a free–dom to cut the strips in interesting curving lines around the guidelines, i.e. measurements, you have set. This is your intent in using this technique. You intentionally do not want to follow rigid marking. You want to guide your scissors so that they cut on either side of these marks as illustrated.

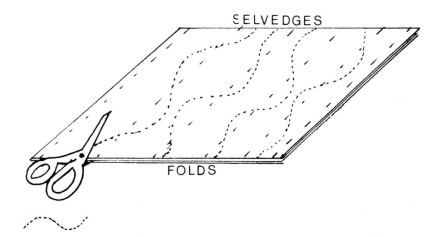

Suggestions for direction of scissors around guideline marks in RANDOM curved strip–piecing

Figure 5.6

RANDOM Method – Inner Strips

EXAMPLE: If you wish to work with the approximate measurement of a finished width 1″ strip, plus ¼″ + ¼″ seam allowance = 1½″, then measure, preferably with a see–through plastic ruler, along the width of the strip from the fold to the selvedge and from the marked guideline of the first or outer strip measurement on your top fabric. Leave very light marks across every 6″ or so just as a guide. Use marking devices that are

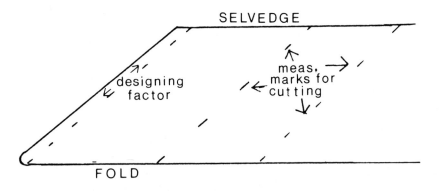

Measured guideline marks for cutting in RANDOM curved strip–piecing

Figure 5.7

removeable as you will be working on the right side of the fabric. These marks are used only as a guide to cutting, not as a guide to sewing. They are on the right side of the fabric and you will be sewing on the wrong side. You may wish to put the marks closer together at first and then use fewer marks as you adapt to the technique. You now have the cutting guidelines for the first inner or second strip in the band. Continue marking the desired measurements for each inner strip in this way.

GRADATED Method – Inner Strips

EXAMPLE: If you wish to work with the finished measurement of $3/4''$ for the first inner or second strip, $1''$ for the second inner or third strip, etc., in the progression of increasing widths, you calculate measurements in this way:

First inner or second strip:
$3/4''$ – finished width
$1/2''$ – seam allowances of $1/4'' + 1/4''$
$1/2''$ – DESIGNING FACTOR
$\overline{1^{3/4}''}$ – TOTAL WIDTH MEASUREMENT FOR GUIDELINE MARKS

Second inner or third strip:
$1''$ – finished width
$1/2''$ – seam allowances of $1/4'' + 1/4''$
$1/2''$ – DESIGNING FACTOR
$\overline{2''}$ – TOTAL WIDTH MEASUREMENT FOR GUIDELINE MARKS

Each fabric is then measured and marked separately at the fold and selvedge only.

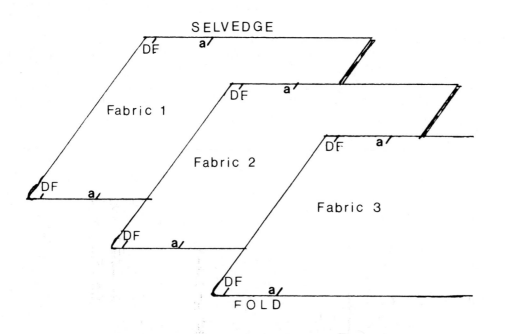

a — Measured guideline marks — GRADATED Method
DF — DESIGNING FACTOR measurement mark

Figure 5.8

B. Cutting the Strips

All cutting of curved strips begins at the <u>fold or centre point</u> of the fabric width, i.e. each fabric is folded in half lengthwise, or doubled selvedge to selvedge, and cut across that width. If you wish to take advantage of a specially printed fabric by cutting parallel to the selvedge (lengthwise), you will have to make adjustments accordingly depending on which method, RANDOM or GRADATED, you are using.

In straight strip–piecing you work from selvedge to selvedge. In Curved Strip–Piecing you work from the centre or fold of the fabric; this is very important for fitting the curves together when assembling. It does not matter how wide the fabrics are, i.e. 90, 115, 122 cm (36, 45, 48″), but it does matter that they are centred on the fold before layering and cutting.

Method of Cutting

Hold the folded fabric layers firmly in one hand and, beginning at the fold, cut with the scissors in the other hand. Do not leave a sharply angled curve when you start cutting. That curve needs to be gently rounded so that it will not pucker when sewn. Remember that the fold will be opened for sewing. A point or line can not be trimmed or straightened out later. After the gently rounded first curve, follow in a freehand motion around the measurement markers you have made. Do not be afraid to let go and vary the distances between the hills and valleys. It is more interesting if there is variety in the frequency of the curves and/or the gradual deepening of the curves. IT TAKES PRACTICE!!

There is a tendency at first not to venture very far from a straight line in cutting so that the appearance of curves in the finished band is minimal. On the other hand, you must be careful not to cut too much of an exaggerated curve because of the problem of sewing that curve without puckers. Cut, shaping a gradual curve, one that does not plunge into a curve and right back out. Remember how difficult extreme curves are to manage on the sewing machine. Seams are not clipped in Curved Strip–Piecing to ease the curves. This would weaken the seams and take too much time. Practice is the best teacher and will lead you to further experimentation. When cutting the second, third, etc. strips, try to vary the opposing curve. Do not make all the strips alike unless you deliberately want that effect.

Suggestions for Cutting Curves

Figure 5.9

You are free to work this technique in any way you wish. The only limitation is how 'curvy' the strips can get and still appear flat or unpuckered in the finished curved strip–pieced band. If a very exaggerated curve is needed, obviously it will have to be appliquéd or shaped with a curving template. It is important to realize both the wonderful possibilities of Curved Strip–Piecing and the limitations of any quiltmaking technique.

C. Preparing the Strips for Sewing

This is one of the most important steps in Curved Strip–Piecing. As the strips are cut, place each unfolded strip beside the next strip in the order cut, i.e. Strip One beside Strip Two beside Strip Three, etc. Do not pile them one on top of the other or open them out flat. Make sure that the curves fit one into the other. If you do get the strips out of sequence, the curves will not match, they will not fit together. You will then have to reconstruct the order in which you cut your fabrics. Remember, the strips are not interchangeable!

If you have chosen RANDOM Curved Strip–Piecing follow the directions for separating the strip layers into the individual curved strip–pieced bands.

If you have a planned sequence of curved strips, follow the directions for GRADATED Curved Strip–Piecing.

D. Sewing the Strips Together to Form the Strip Band

1) Seam Allowance Considerations

As in all piecework, the usual seam allowance is $\frac{1}{4}''$. However, with Curved Strip–Piecing there is built–in flexibility. You are working with a strip of fabric which does not have a straight edge, i.e. a woven thread to come loose, to unravel and fray. In Curved Strip–Piecing there will be some areas along the curved line of the strip which will tend to flatten or straighten out, but the overall outline shape will curve or move toward the bias of the fabric where threads do not tend to come out easily or to fray. This means that where the curve of the strip is more exaggerated (the hill or valley is steeper), a narrower seam allowance can be used to ease that shape. Unlike straight strip–piecing where it is important to have an accurate $\frac{1}{4}''$ seam allowance along the entire strip and maintain the same width measurement, Curved Strip–Piecing, because of the curves which vary all along the strip, by its very nature is not the same width along the strip. This also means the seam allowance can be adjusted to assist in easing the curves for a smoother fit. However, I have found, based on using an average weight of firmly woven broadcloth, that a seam less than $\frac{1}{8}''$ can result in seam separation. Thus, as much as possible, work with a seam allowance of $\frac{1}{4}''$ as you have calculated in your measurements. However, realize that you can modify it up to $\frac{1}{8}''$ and sew a narrower seam where the depths of your curve indicate that it is necessary but do not seam less than $\frac{1}{8}''$ for safety's sake. You will find this 'rule of thumb' especially helpful when you are sewing narrow strips.

Another reason that the narrower seam allowance is possible is that the tension on the fabric threads and the sewing thread along the whole strip is very different between straight and Curved Strip–Piecing. In straight strip–piecing, if the strips are cut and sewn accurately, the seam will be even with the fabric construction threads along the whole sewn strip length, i.e. if you pull tightly side–to–side the tension will be felt evenly along the whole strip. If you pull on a band of Curved Strip–Piecing, that passage of inner tension does not occur because the seam is not straight but crosses the woven construction of the fabric both on the bias and on the straight cross threads. Because of this, certain areas of the strip will tolerate a narrower seam allowance and not separate. This is especially important when the wholly constructed design project is under tension in a quilting frame, and when the strip band is used in long shapes or large areas. You will find this flexibility in sewing the strips very helpful.

2) <u>Pinning</u>

In Curved Strip–Piecing there is a definite order to the fitting together of the strips for seaming. Each curve must fit into the shape of the strip piece to be sewn to it. If the cutting is done properly, there should be no problem.

I find it easiest to work the sewing and pinning of the strips together from my lap as I am sitting at the sewing machine. If I have arranged the strips in order in an area away from my sewing machine, I often slide them onto my cutting mat. For each band, keep all strips in their CORRECT cutting order next to each other, and place one band next to the machine ready for sewing. DO NOT DROP THE STRIPS OR STACK THEM OUT OF ORDER! Remember that each curve is cut and arranged to fit into the curve opposite.

Sitting at the sewing machine, pick up the first folded outside strip and open it out on your lap with the right side up and the centre or fold of the fabric placed in the centre of your lap; the rest of the strip hangs down on either side of you. The curved cut edge of the strip should be toward the sewing machine, the straight edge parallel to your body. Pick up the second strip which will have curved edges on both long sides (unless there are only two strips in the band). Watch carefully to remember which side will fit into the curved edge of the first strip on your lap. Open the fold; place this second strip against the first strip matching up the folds and fitting the matching curves into each other as a check to be sure it is the correct strip. Then turn this strip over, right side down, on top of the first strip, aligning the centre fold. Pin where the hills and valleys meet, pinning from the centre. Where the valley or concave curve of one strip is seen, behind it should be the hill of the other strip to which it is to be seamed.

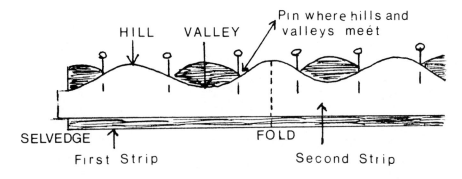

Figure 5.10

The strips will not be mirror images of one another; where one curved strip has concave curves (valleys), the other has convex curves (hills). They will only meet where those points intersect. Remember you are working with Curved Strip–Piecing! Do not try to straighten them out!

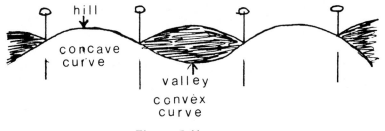

Figure 5.11

With long straight pins, pin the two strips together where the hills and valleys meet starting from the centre out to each side. Continue across the strip to each end. As you become more experienced you may elect to pin the meeting place of every second hill and valley. PINNING IS NECESSARY. If the fabrics are not held firmly at this common meeting spot, the strip will slowly stretch along the seamline shifting the curves. Rippling and puckering will result and grain line direction will be altered. If you find this happening when sewing, stop, rip your stitching out to where the problem begins, re–pin and sew more carefully. When inserting the last pins at the selvedge edges, you may find that the selvedges are not even. This usually is because fabrics of different widths have been used. It does not matter in this technique. In fact, it happens more often than not. What matters is that you align the strips and pin from the centre.

3) Sewing

Begin by machine sewing the first two strips together, starting at the left selvedge in front of the first pin and where the first curves of the strips meet. Do not worry if selvedges are not even. Sew from one selvedge along the seamline to the other edge. It is also possible to sew from the centre to one end, and then from the centre to the other end. However, if the strips are pinned together correctly it is easier and less time–consuming just to sew one long seam.

As you sew, guide the pinned strips under the needle carefully by using your hands in front of the presser foot; your right hand to manipulate the underneath strip, your left hand to direct the top strip. In the seaming, I find I use the thumb and first finger of my right hand (I am right–handed) to hold the bottom strip in order to 'persuade' it gently to move slightly to the right, especially the valleys or concave curves. I also tend to push or move the top strips lightly toward the needle.

As you guide your curves through the presser foot and needle, do it without tension or pulling. Lift the presser foot every few inches or whenever you wish to loosen the fabrics and straighten out the direction of the sewing. You will be surprised how the fabrics will adjust to this manoeuvering. You have to experiment and find what works best for you. Join all the strips together by following this same procedure of assembling, pinning and sewing. Remember, always start aligning and pinning from the centre of the strips.

NOTE: If you do not believe in pinning, you will find it difficult to sew strips together without some pulling and manipulating which, by the time you reach the end, will have thrown the meeting places of your hills and valleys out of alignment. The band will be puckered and wrinkled. If this happens, check to see if the hills and valleys fitted exactly into each other. That is usually the biggest cause of puckering. When sewn together, the strips should appear as smooth and unpuckered as straight strip–piecing. Some fabrics may be more difficult to work with which might cause a problem. There is the possibility that you might want some 'texture' on your surface design and the puckering might just do that! However, puckering along the seam is not truly what Curved Strip–Piecing should look like. If it is there in the finished piecing, the act of quilting will not eliminate the problem or flatten the surface.

You will be surprised at how manageable the fabrics are, especially 100% cotton. We tend to think of our woven fabrics as being difficult to manipulate, and curves and biases being something to avoid. The Curved Strip–Piecing technique will change both these perceptions. There is a mobility in the fabrics, especially 100% cotton, which makes Curved Strip–Piecing work. This time in piecework, having a curving shape with some bias direction allows the fabrics to be manipulated by your hands under the sewing needle so that an unpuckered seam results. You are using to advantage what you had previously avoided.

Sew all the strips together and complete the strip band before pressing it. It is easier to iron the whole band at one time to direct the seams, and to press flat. Ironing before the band is complete will distort or stretch the exposed curved edges of the unsewn fabric strip.

E. Pressing the Strip Band

When all the strips are sewn together, you are ready to press the curved strip–pieced band. With the iron set at the correct temperature for your fabrics, press very lightly on the wrong side first. Place your band on the ironing board, seams and seam allowances facing you, and iron all seams to one side. Do not press heavily with the iron as you are just trying to get all the seams going in the same direction. Press one small area, lift the iron, move it to another area, and press again. Do not try to glide the iron right across the surface. This is one technique where it is not possible to press the seams open; you would have great difficulty maintaining the curved shape and eliminating puckering.

After stabilizing the seams in one direction on the wrong side of the band, turn the band over, right side facing up with the seam allowances directed away from you. Place the band lengthwise, parallel to the ironing board surface. With your left hand (if you are right–handed, or vice versa) hold the left end of the band and firmly but lightly tug as the other hand moves the iron under pressure across the band. This slight tension while ironing will reduce or eliminate puckering and aid in a smooth curved appearance to your band. Check as you iron for any errors in seaming, i.e. tucks, too narrow a seam allowance, etc., and take time to redo the stitching before the final pressing. If you find there is an error which is very difficult to eliminate, but you are planning to cut your band up into other shapes, you may choose to work around this one spot if it is not worth the time to resew.

Take care with the pressing – you will have a much smoother result. This will heighten the appearance of the rounded curved shapes you have cut and sewn. Remember that polyester blend fabrics require additional care because once a crease or fold is pressed or heat set with an iron, it is difficult if not impossible to remove. One hundred percent cottons adjust to heat and pressing very well, and should give you few problems.

F. Marking, Cutting and Sewing Design Shapes

When the assembling and pressing is complete, you are ready to use your curved strip–pieced band with the geometric shapes of traditional patchwork. If using a straight linear configuration, you may elect to measure and mark with a ruler and pencil. However, it is probably still best to make a template for the desired shape. I have found it more accurate to use a template with no seam allowance as you do in hand–piecing. Because the template is the actual size of the pattern piece, I can move this shape around on the curved band and see exactly what the finished shape will look like. Also, I am aware of the visual impact at my seam line, and what its appearance will be when joined to the next fabric shape.

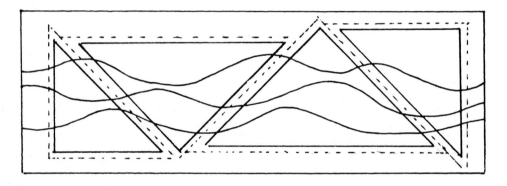

Figure 5.12

To mark your strip band, place the template on the wrong side of the band, right side down. Move it in different directions until you get the design effect you want; especially watch to take advantage of the most effective combination of curves. Make use of the additional fabric, added to both outside edges by the DESIGNING FACTOR, to vary the visual image. When you are satisfied, trace lightly around the template with a marker. Remember to place these shapes on the band leaving ½″ between templates to allow for ¼″ seam allowances when you cut. Follow these marked lines with your sewing machine needle when you assemble the pieces. They should all fit accurately if they were marked correctly. Match up the corners and the edges accurately. Follow the usual quiltmaking procedures to complete your design and the quilting.

SPECIFIC DIRECTIONS

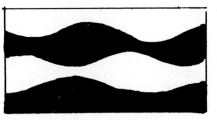

6

Up to this point, the Basic Curved Strip–Piecing Formula has been outlined and then discussed step–by–step in detail. Now we will look specifically at the two methods of Curved Strip–Piecing with explicit directions to follow for each technique.

METHOD I – RANDOM Curved Strip–Piecing

Method I is called RANDOM which indicates that there is no preplanned or specifically desired visual order to the placement of each strip of fabric in the strip–pieced band – no definite order next to each other of pattern, colour or width. It is RANDOM in grouping. The finished curved strip–pieced band will give the overall effect of the fabrics and colours selected, i.e. the random blues of the sky or sunset colours. This is the simpler of the two methods and is less time–consuming as far as the actual cutting procedure because all chosen fabrics are cut at one time.

A) For Two Fabrics – Repeated in Alternating Sequence
1) Selecting the Fabrics

Select two fabrics for this method. If you desire a definite emphasis in the appearance of your curves within the strips use two contrasting colours, i.e. complementary colours or contrasting values of one colour such as light and dark. For a subtle design effect, i.e. a visual blending of your curves one into the other, consider choosing like values of analogous colours, or close values of monochromatic colours.

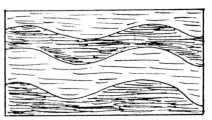

Contrasting values

Close values

Figure 6.I.1

29

2) Preparing the Fabrics

Using your clear plastic ruler and a sharp rotary cutter, straighten or align the crossgrain edges across the entire width of each selected fabric from fold to selvedge. This will give you a straight edge from which to measure.

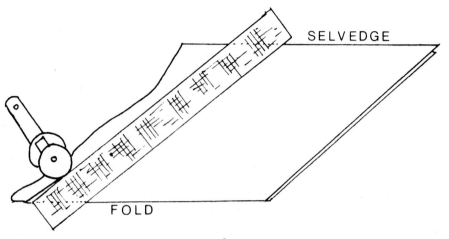

SELVEDGE

FOLD

Figure 6.I.2

3) Layering the Fabrics

In the RANDOM method of Curved Strip–Piecing all fabrics are stacked one on top of the other for marking and cutting. Place the darker fabric, fold toward you, right side up on a flat surface. Place the second, lighter–coloured fabric on top of the first fabric, evenly covering and aligning your crossgrain edge with that of the first fabric. (The lighter fabric is on top to see more clearly the guideline marks which will be made before cutting.) Be sure to line up the folded edges one on top of the other very carefully and accurately. You may wish to pin through all layers first if necessary to hold in place. You will find that the fabrics tend to hold together on their own. Do not worry if the selvedges do not meet. The folds must meet exactly because you will begin cutting curves from there. This is Curved Strip–Piecing!

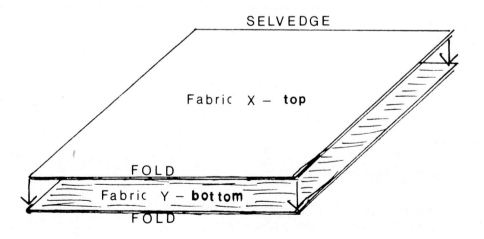

SELVEDGE

Fabric X — **top**

FOLD

Fabric Y – **bottom**

FOLD

Figure 6.I.3

4) <u>Marking the Layered Fabrics</u>

Because the fabrics are stacked one on top of the other, it is necessary to make guideline measurement marks on the top fabric only.

a) <u>Outer or First Strip</u>

Use the measurements you have calculated for the first strip from the Basic Curved Strip–Piecing Formula, i.e. the desired approximate finished width of the strip plus the seam allowances of ¼″ each side = ½″ plus the DESIGNING FACTOR of at least ½″. Mark very lightly about every 6–8″ across the top fabric along the straightened edge, fold to selvedge.

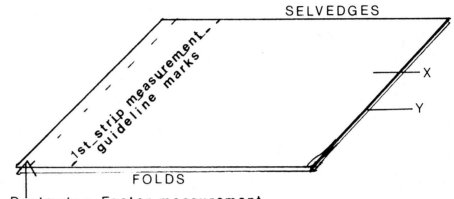

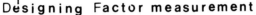

Figure 6.I.4

b) <u>Inner or Second Strip</u>

Using the measurement figure you calculated for the second strip, i.e. the approximate finished strip width plus seam allowances of ¼″ + ¼″, lightly mark your guideline points for cutting the second strip by measuring from the dotted line across the top fabric formed by the guideline marks of the first strip. You will now have 2 rows of marking.

c) <u>Third Strip and All Other Inner Strips</u>

Know the desired measurements and mark in the same way as the first inner strip.

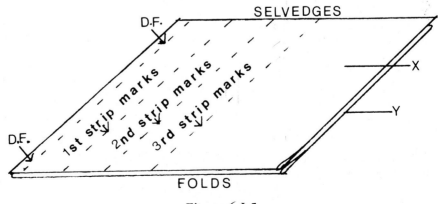

Figure 6.I.5

d) Outer or Last Strip

The guideline marks for the last strip should be calculated from the approximate desired width measurement plus the seam allowances of $\frac{1}{4}'' + \frac{1}{4}''$ plus the DESIGNING FACTOR of at least $\frac{1}{2}''$.

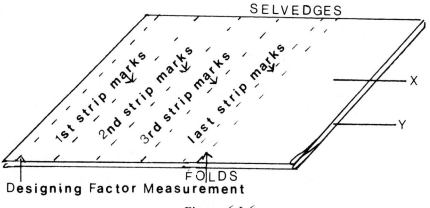

Figure 6.I.6

You now have your layers of fabrics with the top one marked to aid you in designing curves with your scissors. The marks may look further apart vertically than you envisioned your band width to be, but remember they include seam allowances and, with the outer strips, the DESIGNING FACTOR.

5) Cutting the Layered Fabrics
   a) Outer or First Strip

Hold the two layers of fabric firmly in your hand and prepare to freehand cut through both the fabrics with your sharp scissors in a curving motion. Begin cutting at the FOLD. Do not make a sharp-angled cut, i.e. sharply down or up, at the start, cut in a straight line for $\frac{1}{4}''$ then gradually move into a curve so that

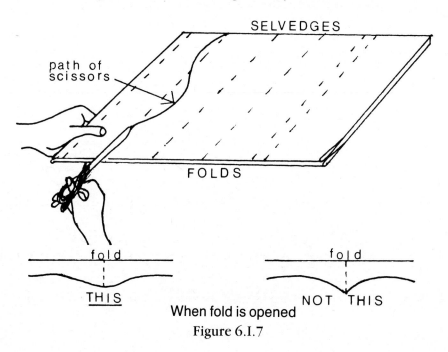

When fold is opened

Figure 6.I.7

1

"Discoveries"
Marilyn Stothers, 1983
48"/122cm. × 48"/122cm.
Curved Strip–Piecing used in triangle
shapes for design of quilt.
(See page 65 PROJECT)

2

Detail

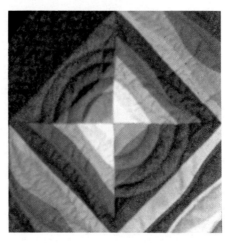

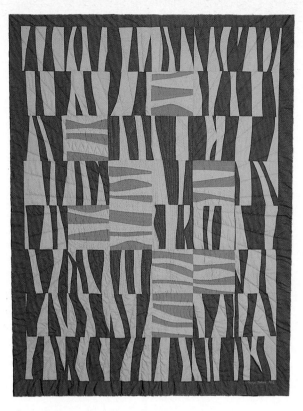

3

Heaven And Earth
Marilyn Stothers, 1983
70"/178cm. × 90"/229cm.
First quilt made using Curved Strip–Piecing.

4

Detail

5

Phoenix Vision
Valerie Hearder, Mahone Bay, N.S., 1985
58"/147cm. × 38"/96cm.
Curved Strip–Piecing used in areas of surface design.

6

Reflections And Illusions I
Marilyn Stothers, 1984, 64"/163 cm. × 34"/86 cm.
Contrasting Curved Strip–Piecing and straight strip–piecing. First in a series of five.

7

Reflections And Illusions IV
Marilyn Stothers, 1986.
53"/135 cm. × 55"/140 cm.
Fourth in a series using circles and squares.

8

Reflections And Illusions III
Marilyn Stothers, 1985.
49"/125 cm. × 49"/125 cm.
Curved Strip–Piecing used
within the circular area
(Private Collection)

9

Reflections And Illusions V
Marilyn Stothers, 1988
65"/165 cm. × 81"/205 cm.
Curved Strip–Piecing used
within circular shape — this
time Curved Strip–Piecing is cut
and sewn in two directions.

10

Curving Cubes II
Marilyn Stothers, 1985
74"/188 cm. × 74"/188 cm.
The cubes progress across the quilt diagonally in
Curved Strip–Piecing and/or similar hand quilting
design.

11

Back

12

Detail

13

Traditional Blocks using Curved Strip–Piecing. **Eight Pointed Star**, **Lone Pine Tree**, **Roman Stripes**.

14

Details of Curved Strip–Piecing used in quilts by Marilyn Stothers.

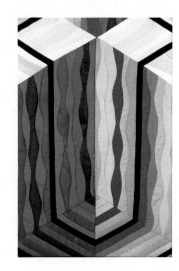

15

"Mommy, Will There Always Be Flowers?"
Marilyn Stothers, 1986, 72"/183 cm. × 52"/132 cm.
An allegorical quilt. Curved Strip–Piecing used in 'grass' image.

16

Back

17

Detail

Cheryl Amor
Lismore, N.S.W., Australia

Suzanne Dowsett
Perth, W.A., Australia

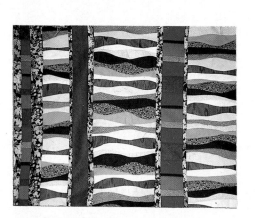

Viive Howell
Bauckham Hills, N.S.W., Australia

Leonie Harrison
Tathra, N.S.W., Australia

Cathy Day
Caringbah, N.S.W., Australia

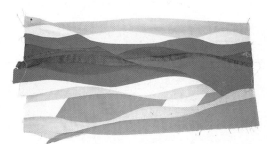

Anne Whitsed
St. Johns Wood, Qld., Australia

18

Projects begun by students in Workshops on Curved Strip–Piecing taught by Marilyn Stothers at the Quilters and Patchworkers of New England 1988 Bicentennial Quilt Symposium, Armidale, New South Wales, Australia.

b) <u>Inner or Second Strip</u>

Separate the next fabric strips, still folded, right side of fabric facing you. Place Fabric X (top fabric) against Fabric Y's (bottom fabric) Strip One, matching and fitting into the cut curves. Take Fabric Y (bottom fabric) and place against Fabric X's (top fabric) Strip One. Match the hills and valleys. Be very careful not to reverse the direction of the strips especially if using plain broadcloth.

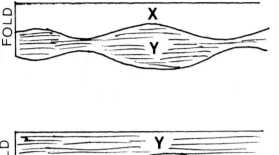

Figure 6.1.12

c) & d) <u>Third Strip, All Other Inner Strips and Outer or Last Strip</u>

Follow the same procedure of patterning and continue sys-tematically alternating the placement of Fabric X and Fabric Y until all strips are placed in their designated order and you have now 2 curved strip–pieced bands of 2 alternating fabrics to sew.

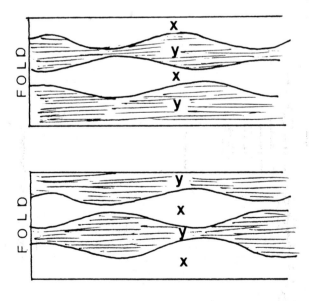

Figure 6.1.13

7) <u>Sewing the Strip Band</u> (see page 26)

Follow the pinning and sewing directions as outlined on page 26 for sewing all the strips together. DO NOT IRON EACH STRIP AS YOU GO. Do the ironing of the whole band at one time when all the strips are sewn together.

8) <u>Pressing the Strip Band</u> (see STEP 6 – F. <u>Pressing the Strip Band</u> on page 27)

This completes Band 1. Band 2 is assembled, pinned, sewn and pressed in the same manner. You now have two bands of the same fabrics in the RANDOM Curved Strip-Piecing method. They should look like the following illustrations.

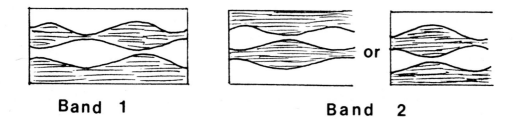

Band 1   **Band 2**

Figure 6.I.14

Or, if you turned the second band upside down, you would have 2 bands that look similar. These may be sewn together end–to–end to make one long continuous band, or lengthwise to make a very wide band. See Method II – GRADATED Curved Strip-Piecing for directions on joining bands together lengthwise.

B) **For Three or More Fabrics – in Random Sequence**

1) <u>Selecting the Fabrics</u>

For this method, select three or more fabrics. In selecting the number of fabrics to use, you must also make a decision regarding the number of strips you wish in your finished curved strip–pieced band. You may choose as few as three fabrics and use several fabrics more than once, i.e. for five strips within the band. This means that after cutting across the three stacked fabrics five times (4 curving cuts and the fifth or last cut straight), you will have 5 strips of each fabric. When sewn together in the RANDOM Curved Strip–Piecing method they will give you 3 curved strip–pieced bands, each with a different appearance in the arrangement of your 3 chosen fabrics.

NOTE: In the RANDOM Curved Strip–Piecing method, the number of curved strip–pieced bands resulting after cutting and sewing will be equal to the number of fabrics you have selected, i.e. if you chose 3 fabrics to work with, you will have 3 curved strip–pieced bands to assemble and to use in designing. The number of strips within the band will be equal to the number of designing cuts made as you 'curve' across the layered fabrics.

Number of fabrics selected = number of curved strip–pieced bands resulting when strips are sewn together

Number of strips within curved strip-pieced band = number of cuts made across fabric layers

2) Choosing the Colours

In the colour selection of three or more fabrics for RANDOM placement, decide if you want visually contrasting curved strips. In this case, try complementary colours with strong value differences in one hue. Perhaps you desire a blending or a subtle shading of colours. You might try colours next to each other on the colour wheel or hues of like values. Remember that each finished band will contain a different fabric combination, i.e. different in order or placement of one next to the other.

3) Preparing the Fabrics

Follow the directions of A) 2).

4) Layering the Fabrics

Following the directions of A) 3), layer the additional fabrics in the same manner as the second fabric. I would advise not selecting more than 5 fabrics, and then only if you have very sharp scissors. When I discuss the GRADATED Curved Strip-Piecing method, I will tell you how to join one band to another band. This will then allow you to have as many fabrics as you want in one larger curved strip-pieced band without having to cut through an unwieldy stack of fabrics at one time. It may be difficult to pin all fabrics together but you will find that most fabrics hold themselves together and, with care, do not slip apart. Again, do not worry if the selvedges do not meet or line up together. It is the centre folds of all fabrics that must be even and exact.

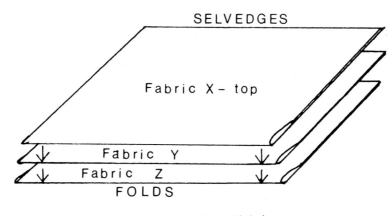

SELVEDGES

Fabric X – top

Fabric Y

Fabric Z

FOLDS

Layering 3 fabrics

Figure 6.1.15

5) Marking and Cutting the Layered Fabrics

Keeping in mind that you are working with more than two fabrics, follow the directions of A) 4) and A) 5) for:
a) Outer or First Strip
b) Inner or Second Strip
c) Third Strip and All Other Inner Strips
d) Outer or Last Strip

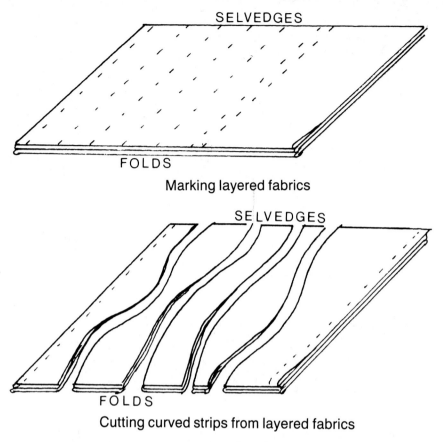

SELVEDGES

FOLDS

Marking layered fabrics

SELVEDGES

FOLDS

Cutting curved strips from layered fabrics

Figure 6.I.16

6) **Assembling the Fabric Strips in Preparation for Sewing the Strip Band**

THIS MUST BE DONE IN EXACT ORDER!

a) **Strip One – Outer or First Strip**

Separate the 3 or more fabrics cut by placing the first or top fabric, Fabric X, still folded, in front and ahead of you on a flat surface. Place the second fabric, Fabric Y, still folded, parallel to the first fabric and below it by about 10″. Place the third fabric, Fabric Z, another 10″ or so below and parallel to the first 2 fabrics. Continue in this same manner if you have more than 3 fabrics.

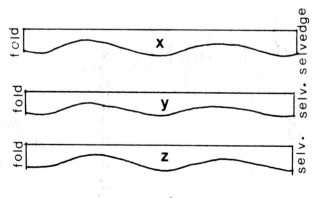

Figure 6.I.17

b) <u>Strip Two – Inner or Second Strip</u>

Lift up the top fabric, Fabric X, from the second strip pile and, while it is still folded, you have the choice of placing it against the matching curves of the first strip of Fabric Y or Fabric Z. Choose one. Take the second fabric, Fabric Y of the same second strip, stack and place the matching curved edge against either Fabric X or Fabric Z. If 3 fabrics have been used, the third fabric, Fabric Z from the second strip pile, will then be placed against the remaining first strip.

In each case, match the hills and valleys, have the right side of the fabrics facing up, and be careful not to get out of sequence.

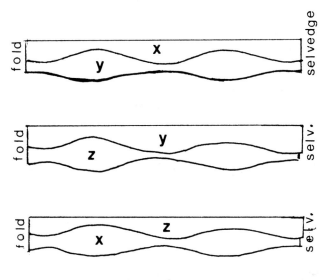

Figure 6.I.18

c) & d) <u>Strip Three – Third Strip, All Other Inner Strips and Outer or Last Strip</u>

Continue in the same manner of separating the strip layers, always varying the placement choice of fabrics so that the same fabrics are not next to each other. You may find that you have a choice here of being completely RANDOM or of having some slight order within the placement.

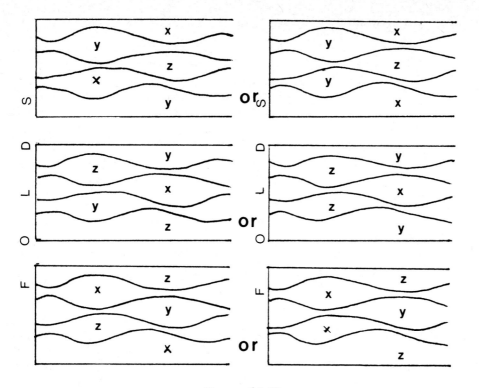

Figure 6.I.19

There are many arrangements you may choose. Also, the com–pleted bands may be turned around. This gives another and different perspective. Remember this is RANDOM Curved Strip–Piecing.

7) Sewing the Strip Band

Follow the directions on page 26, in this case with 3 or more fabrics, and 3 or more bands.

8) Pressing the Strip Bands

Follow the directions on page 27.

METHOD II – GRADATED Curved Strip–Piecing

Choose this method for a planned specific arrangement or order for the curved strips within your band. You may need a controlled gradation of colour, i.e. lights to darks in value changes; or a series of varying widths such as wide to narrow or a combination of widths, etc. This method is the one I seem to use more often because it gives me control over the appearance of my completed strip band and thus the whole surface of my work. The difference in technique between the RANDOM and GRADATED methods is in the layering of the fabrics, marking the guideline measurements, and in the cutting. The assembling, sewing, pressing and end use are the same.

1) Selecting the Fabrics

    As many fabrics as you wish to use for planning your special design may be selected for this method. The fabrics are layered only two at a time, not in multiples. If you wish a gradation of colour, select fabrics in the desired colour range and then arrange them in the order you wish to see them in the finished strip band. Play with them and move them around until you are completely satisfied. Do the same planning of the order of your fabrics for strip width variations, and any other specific arrangement you have in mind. This must be done before curve cutting the strips because this order cannot be altered once the strips are cut – each curved strip fits into the contours of the next strip. However, if (in desperation!) there is a need to change after all the strips are cut, I have found that I can use the cut strip I wish to omit as a template and cut another fabric strip in the same shape to insert in the band. I recommend this only as an 'emergency plan' because the cutting is not quite as accurate as the original. Before beginning, it is still best to be as sure as possible about the cutting order of your fabrics.

    In selecting the Curved Strip–Piecing technique for your surface design you may have decided you want a definite emphasis in the shape of your curves within the strip band. Thus the fabrics you select should contrast one with the other either in colour, print vs. plain, texture, etc. If you desire subtle blending of the curves into each other then your fabrics should be close in colour values, similar texture, etc. These considerations will affect the planned order of your fabrics for cutting.

2) Preparing the Fabrics

    Follow the same directions for the RANDOM Curved Strip–Piecing method (page 30).

    3), 4) and 5) are the important steps which mark the difference in technique between GRADATED Curved Strip–Piecing and RANDOM Curved Strip–Piecing. The DESIGNING FACTOR of $1/2''$ is added to the measurement calculations of ALL strips.

3) Marking the Measurement Guidelines

    In the GRADATED method, each fabric is marked with your measurement calculations. These are used as guidelines for layering the fabrics and for curve–cutting with your scissors. Begin by aligning your selected fabrics in the order you wish them to appear in your curved strip–pieced band. Fan them out so that you can see each fabric.

Arranging fabrics

Figure 6.II.1

a) <u>Outer or First Strip</u>

Place the first fabric in your order on a flat surface, fold toward you, right side facing. From the straight crossgrain edge, left side (working from left to right – see illustration), measure the DESIGNING FACTOR of $\frac{1}{2}''$, marking at the fold and at the selvedge only. In the GRADATED method, it is not necessary to make guideline marks all across the fabric. Using the figures you have calculated for the first (outer) strip, from the Basic Curved Strip–Piecing Formula, i.e. the desired approximate finished width of the strip plus the seam allowances of $\frac{1}{4}''$ each side $= \frac{1}{2}''$, measure from the DESIGNING FACTOR marks and lightly make a second set of marks at the fold and the selvedge. Set this fabric aside.

b) <u>Inner or Second Strip</u>

Take the second fabric in your planned order, follow the same measuring and marking directions as for the first strip. First mark the DESIGNING FACTOR of $\frac{1}{2}''$, then mark the strip width measurement plus seam allowances. Set this fabric aside.

c) <u>Third Strip and All Other Inner Strips</u>

With the third fabric and all consecutive fabrics in your planned arrangement EXCEPT THE LAST FABRIC, follow the same directions as for previous strips.

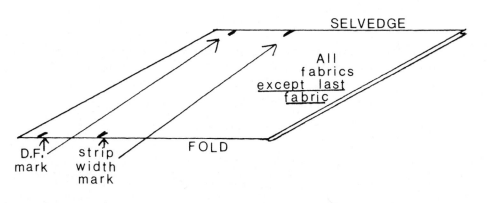

Figure 6.II.2

d) Outer or Last Strip

Measure and mark as for previous strips with the addition of a second DESIGNING FACTOR measurement of $\frac{1}{2}''$ on what will be the outer (unsewn) edge. This last strip will have guideline marks indicating a DESIGNING FACTOR plus the strip width measurement plus seam allowances plus another DESIGNING FACTOR.

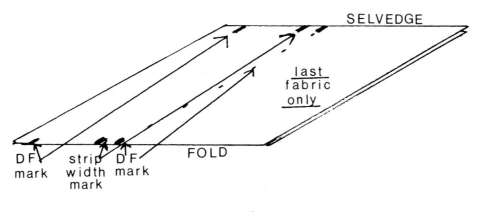

Figure 6.II.3

4) Layering the Fabrics

After all the fabrics are lightly marked at the fold and at the selvedge with the required measurements, assemble them in the sequence you wish them to appear in the finished curved strip–pieced band to reaffirm the order of placement and cutting:

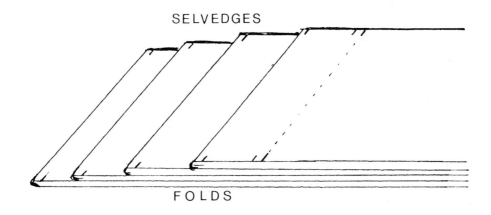

Figure 6.II.4

Taking the first two fabrics, place the first fabric flat on your work–space. Place the second fabric in your planned order, on top of the first fabric, and overlap the second fabric's $\frac{1}{2}''$ DESIGNING FACTOR onto the first fabric's measurement marks made at the fold and selvedge.

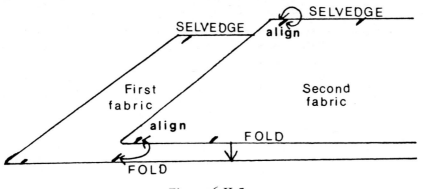

Figure 6.II.5

Align the centre folds of each fabric parallel with the selvedges. Check that the top or second fabric has evenly overlapped the marks on the first fabric by the ½″ all across the fabric width. You may decide to pin at strategic places to hold the fabrics together; however, it is usually not necessary. Follow this same procedure in turn of overlapping with each fabric, including the last fabric. Now you are ready to design curves with your scissors!

5) Cutting the Layered Fabrics

The purpose of overlapping the fabrics within the ½″ DESIGNING FACTOR is to provide an area for cutting the curved strip without losing the approximate finished width measurement.

a) Outer or First Strip

Begin cutting at the centre fold by holding the first two layers of fabrics firmly in your hand. Prepare to freehand cut in a curving motion through the overlapped area of both fabrics. When curving toward the edge where the second fabric overlaps the first, be careful not to cut beyond that edge. Remember, at the start do not make a sharp–angled cut, i.e. sharply down or up, but gradually move into a curve so that when the fold is opened for sewing, the contour will be easier to sew.

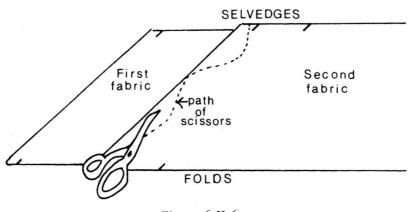

Figure 6.II.6

As in RANDOM Curved Strip–Piecing, think of your scissors as a drawing tool and manipulate them down and up as they cut across the fabrics in a pleasing curving configuration. Set the first cut strip aside, still folded, and discard any small scraps of the second fabric left after cutting in the overlapped area. In GRADATED Curved Strip–Piecing, you will be cutting across one width of fabric, and in the end will have only one set of curved strip–pieced widths to sew together into a pieced band. Remove the unused portion of the first fabric which is underneath the second fabric and set it aside. You are finished with this fabric unless you plan to repeat it in the strip band.

b) Inner or Second Strip

Follow the same procedure of cutting curves as for the first strip, but this time within the overlap of the third fabric on the second fabric. This second cut is where your scissors become the real designing tool – where you have decisions to make regarding the depth, length and direction of your curves. You may wish to follow a repetitive curve sequence (see RANDOM Curved Strip–Piecing, page 41) or be more imaginative and interesting by curving in the opposite direction. You have many choices to enliven your design. Practice will help you with ideas. Remember not to cut closer to the previously cut curve than approximately 1″ (½″ plus seam allowance of ¼″ + ¼″), especially as a beginner with this technique. You might have seaming difficulties. Cut from fold to selvedge.

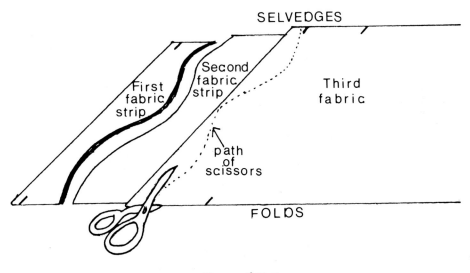

Figure 6.II.7

When you are finished cutting curves across the second strip, set it aside still folded beside the first strip. Remove the second fabric not used which is under the third fabric, just as you did with the first fabric.

c) Third and All Other Inner Strips

Continue designing curves with your scissors as you cut across the two layers of fabric which are overlapped in the same manner as for the previous strips. Remember to remove the fabric from underneath when you are finished cutting.

d) Outer or Last Strip

Curve cut within the overlap of the last fabric and the second from last fabric as previously. Remove the underneath fabric. With a rotary cutter and ruler, cut straight across on the right hand edge of the last fabric following the second DESIGNING FACTOR measurement line.

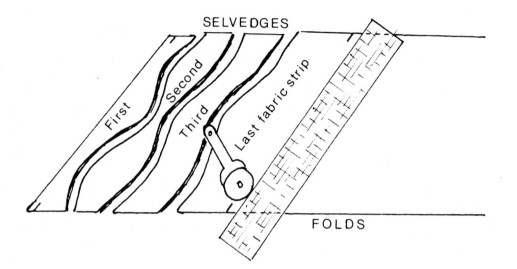

Figure 6.II.8

Keep all folded curved strips against each other as they are cut and check to see they appear as you had planned in your chosen arrangement. Do this before sewing the strips together.

6) Sewing the Strip Band

Follow the same directions as for STEP 6 — D. on page 24.

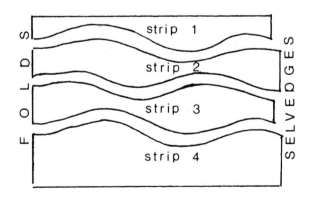

Strips prepared for sewing

Figure 6.II.9

7) **Pressing the Strip Band**

Follow the same directions as for STEP 6 – E. on page 27.

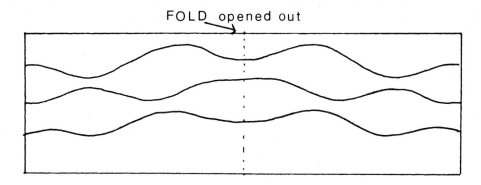

FOLD opened out

Complete GRADATED curved strip–pieced band

Figure 6.II.10

You will now have one GRADATED curved strip–pieced band to work with in designing. If you require more than one band, the same procedure, following steps 1 to 7, is repeated. It is possible to work with 2 layers of the same fabrics each time a strip is cut, resulting in two GRADATED curved strip–pieced bands at one time. The major drawback is that within each band there will be identically shaped curved cuts and the strip contours of each band would appear exactly the same. This may affect your overall surface design detrimentally. I personally prefer a more abstract variety in appearance and so opt for cutting each strip individually.

NOTES

IDEAS FOR PROJECTS

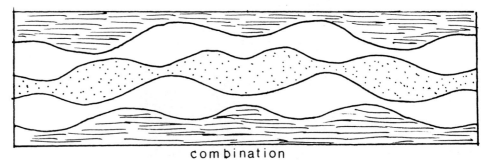

7

Curved Strip–Piecing is a technique for creating 'new fabric' – there is no limit to the number of ideas for projects. Perhaps the following will give you a start.

1. In working with both methods of Curved Strip–Piecing, the appearance of the finished surface design may be varied in the following ways:

    a) Fabric Variations: – use all solid coloured fabrics
                                     – use all subtle printed fabrics
                                     – use a combination of both plain and printed fabrics

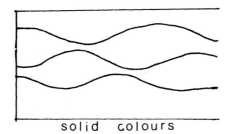

solid colours

printed fabrics

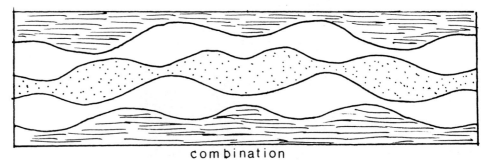

combination

Figure 7.1

b) Colour Variations:
- use analogous colours
- use complementary colours
- use values of one colour

c) Strip Width Variations:
- calculate a different width measurement for each strip
- alternate strips using the same two measurements

Figure 7.2

2. Use both straight strip–piecing and Curved Strip–Piecing in the same project:
- in the same colour and/ or fabric combinations
- in contrasting images

Figure 7.3

3. Use Curved Strip–Piecing in the geometric pattern shapes of traditional quilt blocks.
a) Squares: as in the traditional pattern <u>Rail Fence</u>.

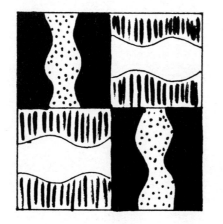

Figure 7.4

b) Rectangles: as part of the surface design or of the border setting of a quilt.

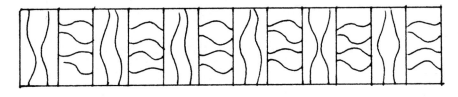

Figure 7.5

c) Triangles: – as in the traditional pattern <u>Roman Stripes</u>

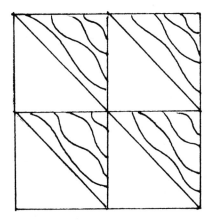

Figure 7.6

– as in the background triangles, i.e. traditional eight–pointed star patterns

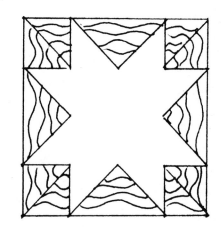

Figure 7.7

– as in an abstract design using a composition of geometric units (see PROJECT, Chapter 9, page 65).

4. Use Curved Strip–Piecing in Seminole patchwork. Here it would be advisable to work in larger measurements as narrow strip–piecing would not use to advantage the visual appearance of the curves in Curved Strip–Piecing.

Figure 7.8

5. Curved strip–pieced shapes, pieced into a design, make an interesting centre focus for a medallion quilt (see PROJECT, Chapter 9, page 65).

6. Scenic designs use Curved Strip–Piecing to great advantage. Subtle colours as well as curving or wavy effects of sky, fields and water are easier to curve strip–piece than applique, and take less time. For contrast, use straight strip–piecing and Curved Strip–Piecing for opposing special effects – straight strip–piecing for the image, Curved Strip–Piecing for reflections.

7. Use Curved Strip–Piecing for abstract, contemporary designing. Here, an excellent colour sense is a real asset because the manipulation of colour images can be very exciting. The soft appearance of the curves enlivens the design (see colour pages).

These are just a few suggestions to get you started. Think of the Curved Strip–Piecing technique and its two methods as producing fabric which you can use in any of the traditional and/or contemporary projects you design.

HAVE FUN, AND HAPPY DESIGNING!

DESIGNING WITH THE GRADATED Curved Strip– Piecing METHOD

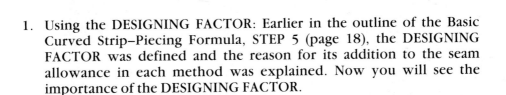

8

1. Using the DESIGNING FACTOR: Earlier in the outline of the Basic Curved Strip–Piecing Formula, STEP 5 (page 18), the DESIGNING FACTOR was defined and the reason for its addition to the seam allowance in each method was explained. Now you will see the importance of the DESIGNING FACTOR.

   When the DESIGNING FACTOR is added to the outer strips of a curved strip–pieced band, you are able to join one band to another band. This will give you a wider band with which to work and additional surface imagery. To join the bands, use the GRADATED Curved Strip–Piecing method of marking, layering and cutting – Steps 3), 4) and 5). With each band becoming a fabric, overlap the ½″ measurement left by the DESIGNING FACTOR on the straight edge of one band on top of the ½″ DESIGNING FACTOR of the second band, and curve cut across the two fabrics.

2. Following Steps 3), 4) and 5), you may also join any shape to another shape using the GRADATED Curved Strip–Piecing method of layering and cutting provided the seam allowances involved have been increased ½″ (equivalent to the DESIGNING FACTOR) before cutting to allow for overlapping. For example, if you wish to join square A to square B with a curved seam, overlap the seam allowances right sides facing up by at least ½″ and curve cut as in the GRADATED method.

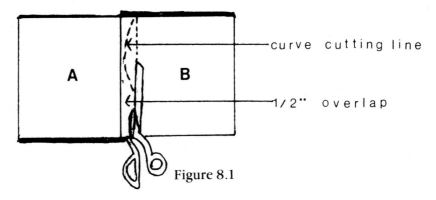

Figure 8.1

3. When fitting together the completed units or larger areas of your design, you may wish to curve each shape into the other. For instance, if I have assembled and sewn a number of curved strip–pieced bands or shapes together and then wish to join one series or large area to another, I will curve cut the edge of one area in a configuration needed to complement what has already been done, and then use this cut edge (mindful of leaving adequate seam allowance) as a template and over-lap, right sides facing, the edge that is to be joined as in the GRADATED Curved Strip–Piecing method and cut following that shape. I then sew these two edges together, which now have hills and valleys, as in all Curved Strip–Piecing.

4. You may think of other wonderful ways to use GRADATED Curved Strip–Piecing!

Try these designs in GRADATED Curved Strip–Piecing with 45° triangles

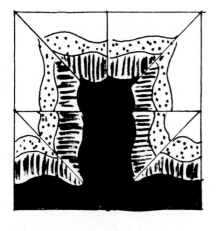

Figure 8.2

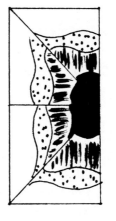 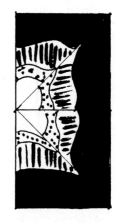

Figure 8.3a   Figure 8.3b

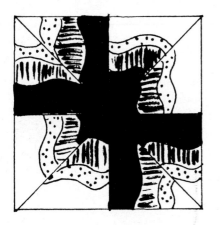   or

Figure 8.4

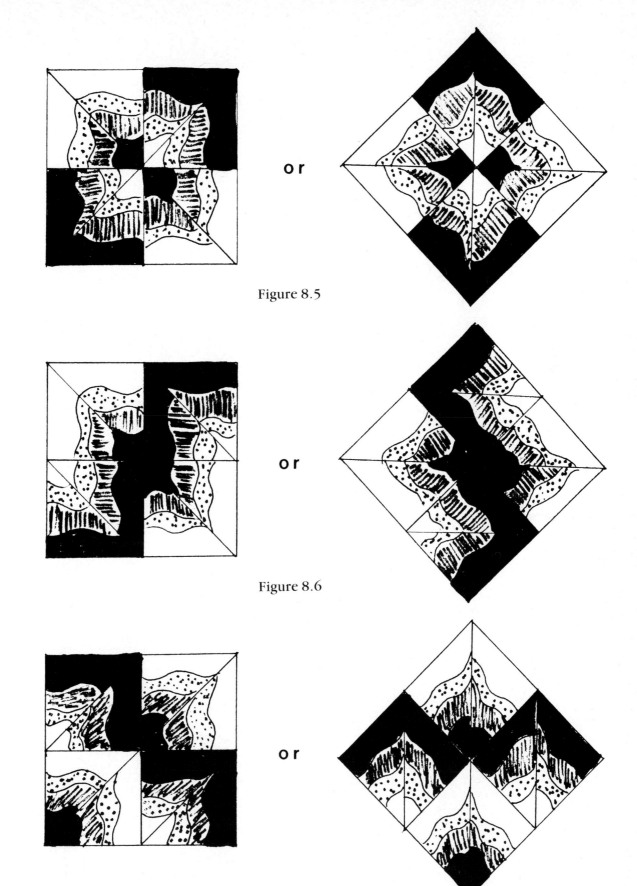

Figure 8.5

o r

Figure 8.6

o r

Figure 8.7

``DISCOVERIES'' QUILT

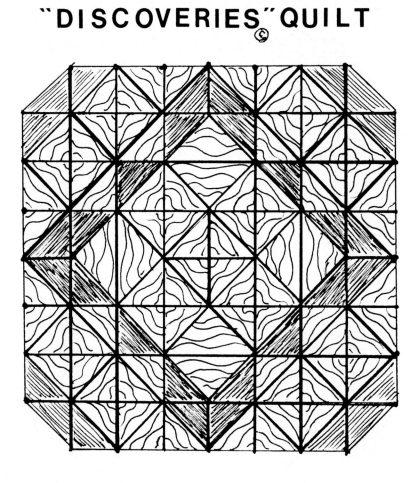

Assembling   Diagram

Figure 9.1

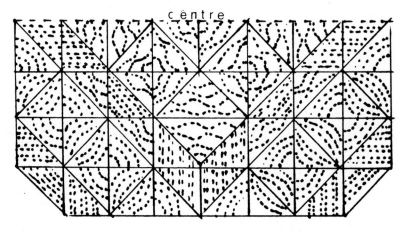

Quilting   Diagram

Figure 9.2

PROJECT:
"Discoveries" Quilt

9

SIZE: 48″ × 48″ (Colour Page 33)

CONTENT:

A. 108   <u>6″ triangles</u> (finished size)

    1. The following triangles are cut from GRADATED curved strip–pieced bands:
       24 light–coloured curved strip–pieced – for top area of quilt
       24 dark–coloured curved strip–pieced – for bottom area of quilt
        8 light–coloured curved strip–pieced – for centre
       12 dark–coloured curved strip–pieced – for centre
       (the centre may be different combinations of light and dark tri-angles)

    2. The following triangles are cut from RANDOM curved strip–pieced bands:
       8 dark–coloured curved strip–pieced – for between the solids of the inner border

    3. 32 dark solid co–ordinating coloured triangles

B. 8   <u>8½″ triangles</u> (finished size)

    8 dark–coloured curved strip–pieced – for between the solids of the inner border (cut from bands made in A.1. and 2.).

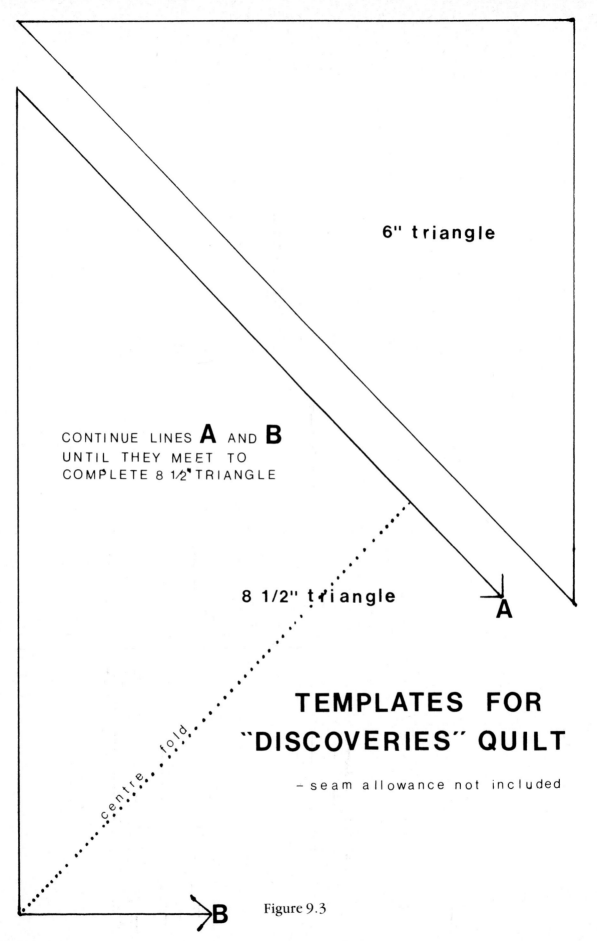

6" triangle

CONTINUE LINES **A** AND **B**
UNTIL THEY MEET TO
COMPLETE 8 1⁄2" TRIANGLE

8 1/2" triangle

A

TEMPLATES FOR
"DISCOVERIES" QUILT

– seam allowance not included

centre fold

B

Figure 9.3

REQUIRED FABRIC: in 2 basic colours and 1 dark co-ordinating solid colour

A. Select 5 values of one colour. As you can see from the colour photograph I have used a flesh-tone beige, deeper beige, light red-brown, red-brown and purple-brown.
Amount of fabric required: at least ⅓ yd (0.3 m.) each of five 44″ fabrics. This will probably allow for extra fabric – it depends on how you arrange your colours.

B. Select 1 contrasting colour. As you see from the photograph I chose blue in 4 values or closely related hues, i.e. light blue, turquoise blue, purple-blue and dark turquoise.
Amount of fabric required: at least ½ yd (0.5 m.) each of four or five 44″ fabrics.

C. Select 1 dark-coloured co-ordinating complementary fabric from which to cut 32 6″ triangles.
Amount of fabric required: ¾ – 1 yd (0.75–1 m.) of 44″ fabric. If you decide to use this fabric for the back of the quilt, buy an additional 1¾ yd (1.75 m.), and then plan the marking and cutting of the triangles so that there is enough length of fabric left for the backing.

METHOD:

A. Construct a number of curved strip-pieced bands in 3 different coloured and/or arranged sequences. The finished width measurement of the curved strip-pieced bands will be based on the following measurements. All triangles in this project are marked and cut in this manner:

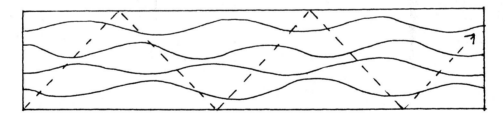

Mark and Cut all triangles as illustrated

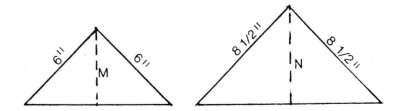

Use measurement M or N for strip band widths

Figure 9.4

"DISCOVERIES" QUILT

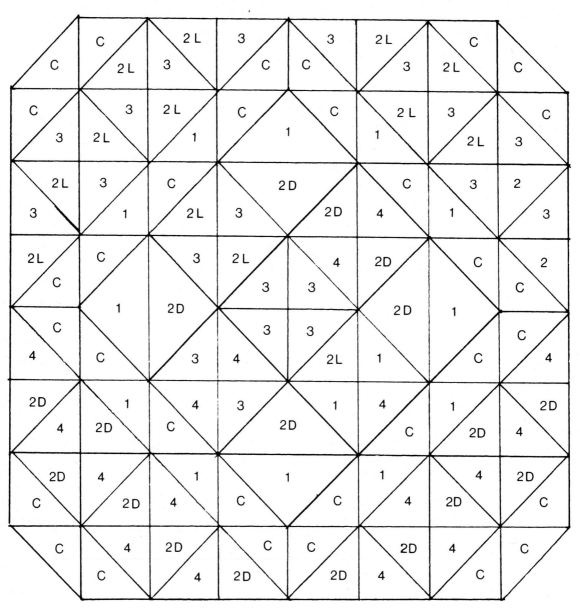

Diagram for placement of triangles
See METHOD for explanation of symbols

Figure 9.5

1. RANDOM Method: Construct one set of curved strip–pieced bands from the fabrics chosen for the second colour sequence. (In the illustration I chose 4 'blue' fabrics.) Layer the fabrics and make 5 cuts (4 curved and 1 straight). Each band (the number of bands will depend on the number of fabrics used) should be composed of 5 curved strips. The width of the finished band should be 6″ plus seam allowances. This is the vertical measurement of the 8½″ triangle from base to point as illustrated. All strip width measurements are then calculated with this in mind (see Figure 9.5 –1).

2. GRADATED Method: Construct six or more bands of 5 curved strips each from the five values of the first colour sequence chosen. Gradation of colour is arranged from light to dark. The width of the finished curved strip–pieced band should be approximately 4¼″ plus seam allowances which is the vertical measurement, base to apex, of the 6″ triangle. The guideline marks for each strip within the band are now calculated from this overall measurement (see Figure 9.5 – 2D–Dark, 2L–Light).

3. GRADATED Method: Following the instructions in 2., construct three or more bands using a combination of light to medium colour value fabrics from the two basic colours you have chosen. The finished width of each band should be approximately 4¼″ (measure your 6″ triangle) plus seam allowances. These are the "light–coloured" bands (see Figure 9.5 – 3).

4. GRADATED Method: Following the instructions in 2., construct three or more bands using a combination of medium to dark colour value fabrics from the two basic colours you have chosen. The finished width of each band should be approximately 4¼″ (measure your 6″ triangle) plus seam allowances. These are the "dark–coloured" bands (see Figure 9.5 – 4).

B. From each completed band, cut several triangles as illustrated and described under CONTENT. Do not mark and cut all triangles at once. Experiment by placing the triangles in various arrangements, moving them around until satisfied with the design. You may wish to work only on the centre area first, then out toward each quarter. Work in the way that suits you best as you explore the design possibilities. As you place one triangle next to another, make use of your curving configurations and their direction within the triangles in order to maximize surface design.

C. Once the areas of light and dark are decided, place the solid triangles as shown in the diagram (see Figure 9.5 – C).

ASSEMBLING:

Following the illustration, assemble the triangles in rows starting at the top row. Join each set of triangles to form a square, then sew one square to the next across to complete the row. Proceed to the next row and repeat the same sewing sequence as for the first row. Continue with each row until all rows of triangles are sewn together. When all rows are complete, join them together in order until the entire quilt top is pieced. Be careful to match all meeting points accurately.

QUILTING

TEMPLATES

FOR "DISCOVERIES" QUILT

Figure 9.6

FINISHING:

Choose a suitable backing fabric – one of the fabrics from the top, or one that co–ordinates with colours used in the surface design. Measure the finished quilt top; backing should be the same size including seam allowances PLUS at least one inch all around (this will allow for any shrinking during quilting). The total measurement should be 50″ square. Select a filling such as bonded polyester or cotton/polyester batting, the same measurements as the backing.

Place backing right side down on a flat surface, being sure that all wrinkles, etc. are smoothed out. Place batting on wrong side of backing, smoothing, centring and aligning to cover backing. Place quilt top, right side up, on top leaving one inch of batting/backing around the edge. Baste all layers together from the centre out to the edges – horizontally, vertically and diagonally. Quilt in the pattern desired. I outline hand–quilted in some areas and in others used a semi–circle design. The solid triangles were quilted with close vertical lines. The colour of the quilting thread may be changed to co–ordinate with the areas you are quilting.

When quilting is completed, finish the outside edges by first trimming off the excess batting and backing. Using the same fabric as for the solid area of the quilt, bind with double bias binding, mitring at each corner. Hand–finish on the reverse or wrong side of the quilt. Do not forget to sign your name and the year of completion! If you plan to hang your quilt, sew a hanging sleeve to the top of the back of the quilt.

NOTES

IMPORTANT POINTS
TO REMEMBER —
A REVIEW

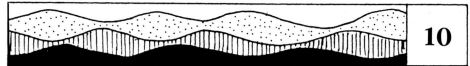

10

1. In the Curved Strip–Piecing technique, you work from the centre fold of each fabric – not from the selvedge.

2. You must make certain that the selvedge is parallel to the folded edge to ensure a straight crosswise grainline.

3. The DESIGNING FACTOR of a minimum of ½″ (more depending on end use) is an essential additional measurement in Curved Strip–Piecing.

4. Your fabric scissors are very important – they are your drawing tool. Curved Strip–Piecing is all about the free–hand cutting of curves.

5. The curved strips, once cut, are not interchangeable. The shape of the curve cannot be changed or altered. Points cannot be rounded, steep curves cannot be softened, areas cannot be trimmed. Each strip configuration, once cut, exactly matches the shape or edge of the strip to which it will be joined.

6. Pin the curved strips together before you sew them, pinning from the centre fold, right sides together, first to one side, then to the other, but only at the common meeting points where the 'hills' and 'valleys' cross over.

7. In sewing together the curved strips, you may use a narrower seam allowance than the usual ¼″ to ease the curves, depending on their depth or steepness.

8. You may use fabrics of varying widths in one band but all must be aligned from the centre fold. If you wish to 'increase' the width of the narrower fabrics before cutting the strips, do the following: From the narrower fabric cut a piece equal to the needed width, sew it to one selvedge and re–adjust to the new centre fold caused by the increased width. You may choose to ignore the seamline of the added–on fabric, or cut around it when using templates. This saves having to make another curved strip band for that necessary one 'patch' or shape that still remains to be cut from the band in order to complete your design.

NOTES

GLOSSARY

CURVED STRIP–PIECING	A technique for the cutting and sewing together of long curved strips of fabric to form a band or 'new' fabric from which to cut template shapes.
Straight Strip–Piecing	A technique for cutting and sewing together long straight strips of fabric to form a band or 'new' fabric from which to cut template shapes.
RANDOM Method	A method of Curved Strip–Piecing followed for an unplanned, haphazard arrangement in the order of the chosen fabrics within the curved strip–pieced band.
GRADATED Method	A method of Curved Strip–Piecing followed for a specific, pre–determined order in the chosen fabrics within the curved strip–pieced band.
DESIGNING FACTOR	A Curved Strip–Piecing term for adding a minimum of ½″ measurement to guideline calculations in both RANDOM and GRADATED methods. See explanation and directions on page 18.
Convex	A shaped line 'rising' from the norm or straight that is curved out or bulging like the outside of a circle or ball.
Concave	A shaped line 'sinking' or dropping down from the norm or straight that is curved inward like the inside of a circle or ball.
Hills	The convex curves in the outline shape of the curved strip.

Valleys	The concave curves in the outline shape of the curved strip.
Gentle Curves	Curves that do not have deep convex or concave shapes, that are freehand cut in Curved Strip–Piecing and assembled with little or no difficulty because they are easily manipulated in sewing.
Exaggerated Curves	Very deep curves not easily assembled in Curved Strip–Piecing; should be avoided in this method. For these curves, use applique or curved templates.
Cut	To form a shape. In Curved Strip–Piecing it refers to a curved strip shape being formed by using scissors (or a sharp cutter) cutting into fabric.
Seam Allowance	The additional measurement, before cutting, of $1/4''$ added to the calculated finished measurements of each horizontal edge of a strip (total $1/2''$) for sewing.
Strip–Pieced Band	When the strips are sewn together they form a band. This becomes the new fabric from which template shapes are cut.
Yardage/Meterage	A yard of fabric is $36''$ in length, a metre is approximately $39''$ in length.
Metric Conversion	1 inch = 2.54 centimeters

MEET THE AUTHOR

Born in Ontario and living in Winnipeg, Canada, Marilyn Stothers has been quiltmaking since 1976. She received her education at MacDonald Institute in Guelph, Ontario, and at Michigan State University from which she graduated. She has taken post–graduate work in Textiles and in Fine Art.

Marilyn began teaching and lecturing in quiltmaking in 1978, first in her own store and then with conferences and guilds in Canada, the United States, Britain, Australia and New Zealand. Many of Marilyn's contemporary quilts have been shown in juried and invitational exhibitions such as Quilt National '85, Visions – San Diego 1987, The Commonwealth Collection 1987, Hands All Around I, II and III, and others where thay have won awards and are pictured in books. She works in original designs, often exploring a theme in a series. From her fabric explorations came the new and original technique of Curved Strip–Piecing which is now used in much of her work. Her workshops usually evolve from her own quiltmaking.

Marilyn presently resides in Winnipeg, Manitoba, with her husband Steve. They have four children.

NOTES